Santiago de Compostela
In the Age of the Great Pilgrimages

St. James the Great, by Albrecht Dürer.

Santiago de Compostela

In the Age of the Great Pilgrimages

By Marilyn Stokstad

Norman : *University of Oklahoma Press*

Library of Congress Cataloging in Publication Data

Stokstad, Marilyn Jane, 1929–
    Santiago de Compostela.

    (The Centers of Civilization Series)
    Bibliography: p.
    Includes index.
    1. Santiago de Compostela—History. 2. Christian pilgrims and pilgrimages—Spain—Santiago de Compostela. I. Title. II. Series.
DP402.S23S77 1978   946'.11   77–18612
ISBN 0–8061–1454–1

To Olaf and Edythe Stokstad
and also Karen, Anna, and Bob

Preface

Today's traveler to the shrine of St. James in Santiago de Compostela cannot but wonder at the isolation of the spot. The city seems far from the mainstream of European activity, and even in Spain it is remote from the centers of political and intellectual life, situated as it is in the far northwest on the Sar River, close to the coast and to Portugal. How difficult it is now to realize that once this sleepy cathedral town, so quiet in spite of its distinguished university and bustling market, was once one of the centers of Christendom. Santiago de Compostela at the beginning of the twentieth century was, in appearance, a beautifully preserved metropolis of the seventeenth and eighteenth centuries. Now scholars and government officials have recognized the value of this happy chance by declaring the entire old town, not just the cathedral building, a national historic monument.

Even by the eighteenth century Santiago de Compostela had ceased to play a major role in world affairs. How did it, then, come to be a center of Christian culture in the Middle Ages? What was its role in the development of European intellectual and social life? In short, what was the contribution of Santiago de Compostela as a city, not just as a religious center, to Western life and thought?

The answer lies in those characteristic movements in the Western medieval world—the Crusades against Islam in the Holy Land and in Spain and the pilgrimages to the shrines of the saints. The period has been analyzed at length by historians, first with emphasis on the spiritual and religious considerations, then with greater attention to the political and economic motivations, and finally with a concentration on the psychology of these mass movements. Attention has focused on the Holy Land for a variety of reasons, not the least of which was the primacy of the Church of Rome. The fact is often forgotten that during the eleventh and twelfth centuries there were three great pilgrimage centers: the Holy Sepulchre in Jerusalem, the shrine of St. Peter in Rome, and the tomb of St. James in Galicia. The pilgrimage and the city of Santiago de Compostela are inextricably bound together. Without the extremely skillful propagandizing of the pilgrimage to the tomb of St. James by the church, especially by the monastic orders, no great city would have developed. Once begun, the city itself became a center of civilization that returned to the pilgrims far more than any of them brought to it.

In studying the role of Santiago de Compostela in the age of the great pilgrimages, I have relied on medieval documents and twentieth-century archaeological studies to give as accurate a picture of the twelfth-century city as possible. In presenting rather free translations of the documents, I hope to catch some of the flavor as well as the sense of the originals.

I wish to thank the directors and staff of the Instituto Padre Sarmiento in Santiago de Compostela, the Instituto Amatller in Barcelona, and the Institute for Research in the Humanities of the University of Wisconsin, and the Spencer Research Library at the University of Kansas for their hospitality and assistance while I wrote this book. I am deeply indebted to the late Jesús Carro García and Manuel Chamoso Lamas in Spain and to Harold and Alice Wethey and Franklin Ludden in the United States for their help. Santiago Alcolea, Montserrat Blanch de Alcolea, José Gudiol, and Dorothy Hughes have consistently encouraged and assisted me in Spain. My studies in Spain have been supported by the American Association of University Women, the National Endowment for the Humanities, and the general research fund of the University of Kansas.

MARILYN STOKSTAD

Contents

		page	
	Preface		ix
	Plan of Medieval Santiago de Compostela		2
I.	Prologue: St. James and Spain		5
II.	The Road to Santiago de Compostela and the Medieval Pilgrimage		14
III.	The Goal of the Pilgrimage: The City and the Cathedral		35
IV.	History and Politics in Santiago de Compostela		64
V.	Social Organization, Economic Activity, and Daily Life in the Twelfth Century		90
VI.	Cultural Life: The Arts and Humanities		131
VII.	Postscript: Santiago de Compostela Through the Centuries		155
	Bibliography		165
	Index		173

Santiago de Compostela
In the Age of the Great Pilgrimages

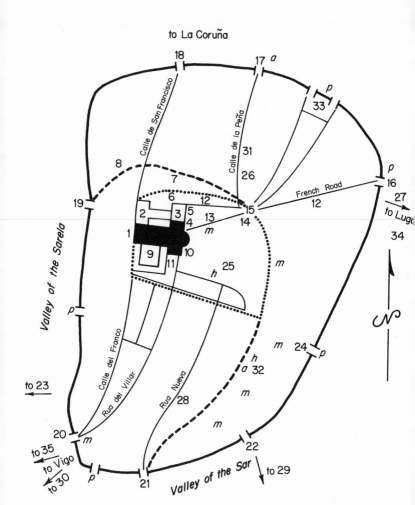

Plan of Santiago de Compostela

Walls: 11th century ....
Extension in mid-11th century
Medieval walls, restored and altered in the 13th, 16th and
19th centuries, now an avenue _ _ _ _ _ _

1. Cathedral of St. James
2. Palace of the Archbishop, with mint and school
3. Paraiso square with fountain and marketplace
4. Church of the Corticela, incorporated into the present cathedral as a chapel
5. Monastery and hospital of San Pelayo Ante-altares
6. Pilgrims' hospital, now site of the Church of St. Martin
7. Monastery of St. Martin
8. Church of the Holy Trinity, hospital and cemetery for pilgrims
9. Cloister of the Cathedral
10. Canons' residence
11. Platerías square, market
12. French Road (Via Francigena)
13. Via Sacra
14. Site of houses belonging to Master Matthew
15. Porta Francigena, gate of the French Road, market square and junction of the Via Sacra and Via Francigena
16. Gate of the French Road, later location (Puerta del Camino, direction: Lugo)

Other gates noted in the *Guide:*

17. Porta Penne
18. Porta de Subfratribus (direction: La Coruña)
19. Porta de Sancto Peregrino
20. Porta de Falgueriis (direction: Padrón and Vigo)
21. Porta de Susannis
22. Porta de Macerellis

Other churches mentioned in the *Guide:*

23. Sta. Suzanna, originally dedicated to the Holy Sepulchre (troops of the Queen and Archbishop assembled here in 1117)
24. St. Felix
25. St. Benedict
26. St. Michel
27. Priory of St. Peter
28. Salome
29. St. Mary by the Sar
30. Church of the Conjo
31. Jewish quarter
32. Ancient and early Medieval fortifications
33. Medieval and 16th century fortifications
34. Leprosarium of Lazarus
35. Leprosarium of St. Martha

a   point of entry of aqueducts
h   other hospitals
m   other market squares
p   postern gates

I.
Prologue:
St. James and Spain

In the Christian tradition James, the son of Zebedee, was called to discipleship by Christ from his life as a fisherman on the shores of Galilee. He was one of the most favored Apostles, and his intimacy with Christ is attested to by the fact that he, with Peter and John, witnessed the Transfiguration of Christ on Mount Tabor. After the Resurrection of Christ, the Apostles, as directed by the Holy Spirit at Pentecost, traveled throughout the world preaching the word of the Lord and converting the people to the Christian faith. According to legend St. James was the apostle to Spain. His place of landing, his itinerary, and the communities he founded were all debated during the Middle Ages and even later. Did he land in Galicia, where he was to return for burial, or would he naturally have landed in the Spanish Mediterranean ports which were busy Roman commercial centers? In any event, the principal miracle associated with St. James's residence in Spain was the appearance of the Virgin Mary in the flesh standing on a stone column. This miraculous event supposedly took place in Zaragoza and is commemorated in the Church of Our Lady of the Pillar, one of the most venerated shrines in Spain.

The legend of the life and miracles of St. James is worthy of our attention because the city of Santiago de Compostela would not have developed as it did if people had not believed in the authenticity of the legend and the relics. After many years of missionary activity, James returned to Jerusalem, where he suffered martyrdom under Herod in A.D. 44. His disciples spirited away his body and (the legend is careful to record) his head, placed his earthly remains in a boat, and set sail from Jaffa. In only seven days the ship, propelled miraculously by wind and waves, arrived at the coast of Galicia. As the ship neared the land, a horseman, riding beside the sea, was carried by his bolting horse into the waves, but instead of drowning, horse and rider came to the surface covered with scallop shells. Henceforth, the scallop shell became the symbol of St. James and the badge of the pilgrim to his shrine.

After St. James's nine apostles landed with their precious burden at Padrón, their first thought was to find a suitable tomb for the saint. A tomb was ultimately provided by a noblewoman named Lupa whose castle and estates lay near by. The tale is recorded in the *Codex Calixtinus,* Book III. Lupa was at first loath to be converted or to welcome the wayfarers; however, she agreed to supply them with oxen to draw the wagon carrying the sarcophagus with the relics of St. James. She directed them to a mountain where the oxen were grazing, expecting to rid herself of the unwelcome petitioners because the beasts were wild and notoriously ferocious. Furthermore, a dragon lurked in a cave on the way. Needless to say, the disciples overcame the dragon, and the oxen, when called upon to bear such a holy burden, became docile at once. Lupa was impressed by the miracle and converted to Christianity. She gave St. James's followers her own family tomb as a sepulchre for the saint. Thus did St. James come to his final resting place in Galicia.

According to the legend the apostles continued on to the Roman city nearby to explain their mission to the ruler. He welcomed them to his palace but secretly intended to slay them. Apprised of his intention, the apostles slipped away, but they were followed in hot pursuit by his men-at-arms. The chase seemed hopeless for the apostles, but as the soldiers pounded across a bridge, it collapsed under them, killing them all and allowing the apostles to continue their journey back to the tomb unmolested.

After the burial of the saint, seven of the apostles traveled throughout Spain as missionaries. Two remained behind, Theodosius and Anastasius, guarding the tomb and ministering to the Christian community which grew up around it. When they died, as witness to their loyalty, they were buried at each side of their master. Shortly thereafter the Christians in Spain as well as in the rest of the empire were persecuted by the Roman emperor Diocletian. The Christian community of Galicia was dispersed, the veneration of the relics of St. James ceased, and the tomb of the saint was forgotten. At the fall of the Roman Empire barbarian Suevi occupied Galicia.

Gradually the Christian community re-emerged in Spain. It thrived first under the Visigothic kingdom, which fell, in turn, to the forces of Islam in the eighth century. Christianity was not completely eliminated in Spain by the Moorish invasion, however, for the Moors were relatively tolerant conquerors. Furthermore, a Christian kingdom was left in the northwest of the peninsula, the Kingdom of Asturias, which flowered under Alfonso II, the Chaste, in the ninth century. In 813 the tomb of St. James was rediscovered. A shepherd, according to a medieval legend, watching his flock by night, saw a star of great magnitude hovering over an oak grove. On investigation the man found a ruined build-

ing. He hurried to report the strange phenomenon to Teodomiro, the bishop of Iria. Bishop Teodomiro went to the
spot and identified the ruins as the tomb of St. James and
his disciples, Theodosius and Anastasius. Thrilled by his
discovery, Teodomiro rushed to the court of Alfonso II in
Oviedo. The King returned with him to the "field of the
star," and thus Alfonso had the honor of being the first
pilgrim to the tomb of St. James at the place which came
to be known as Santiago de Compostela. King Alfonso ordered a church to be built to house the relics. Soon the
episcopal see was transferred from Iria to Santiago de Compostela, and so great became the fame of the shrine that
within a few years a much larger church was needed. Alfonso
III was the next great patron of Santiago, for he ordered
a new church to be built on a very grand scale.

St. James showed his special favor to the Spanish Christians in their struggle to free the country from the Moors
according to another of his most famous miracles. At the
Battle of Clavejo he appeared beside the king to rally the
Asturian soldiers. He rode through the thick of battle in
the guise of a knight on a white charger, trampled the infidel before him, and led the Christians to victory. Thus
he became not only the patron saint of Spain but also of the
Spanish army, which took as its battle cry *"Santiago matamoros."* One of the earliest representations of this theme
is in a tympanum set into the west wall of the south transept
of the present cathedral which shows St. James riding over
the heads of his enemies, sword in hand.

Even with such a patron the city of Santiago de Compostela was not to be left in peace. Vikings raided the coast
but did not destroy the city. But in the tenth century the
Moors under their great general, Almanzor, devastated the
city. The Moors considered Santiago to be to Spanish Chris-

tendom what Mecca was to Islam. Almanzor razed the city but spared the actual tomb of St. James. According to legend, a single monk had remained kneeling in prayer at the tomb, undaunted by the threats of Almanzor's soldiers. Almanzor was so impressed by the old man's steadfastness that he spared him and the tomb he guarded. This tale became very useful in the twelfth century when Toulouse, in competition with Santiago, claimed to have relics of St. James. From that later period also grew the legend that the relics of St. James were miraculously immobile, and thus the monks who guarded them could not even carry them to safety during the Moorish invasions. This story was sufficient evidence to prove to the pilgrims that the only true relics of St. James were located in the Cathedral of Santiago de Compostela. The fury of Almanzor's raid is attested by recent excavations conducted by Sr. Manuel Chamoso Lamas. A layer of ash and rubble covers the site of the churches of Alfonso II and III. Architectural fragments are so tiny as to suggest deliberate, determined, and systematic destruction of the buildings.

The holy relics proved to be not entirely immobile, however; at least Archbishop Diego Gelmírez was able to remove a bone from the skull and present it to the Cathedral of Pistoia in the twelfth century. A tooth was also removed and placed in a special reliquary in the treasury along with the hat, staff, and other equipment of St. James. Later the relics of the saint were taken from their place under the high altar and reburied a few feet behind it when Galicia and the cathedral were threatened by an English army led by Sir Francis Drake. Since the archbishop evidently took charge of hiding the relics himself and left no records, the bones were lost until the end of the nineteenth century although no one realized it.

In a more secular age the decision was made to carry

out a scientific exploration of the tomb of the saint. At the end of the last century, a canon of the cathedral, D. Antonio López Ferreiro, was appointed by the archbishop to carry on the work. The results of López Ferreiro's investigations are published in his monumental eleven-volume study, the *Historia de la Santa A. M. Iglesia de Santiago de Compostela,* which covers the entire history of the building and includes in appendices most of the pertinent documents still in the cathedral archives. Under López Ferreiro's direction, the excavators first entered the tomb chamber, but it was empty and they were unable to locate the relics. Then, noticing a star pattern in the pavement behind the altar, they dug directly under it and found the bones of three men buried together in evident haste and secrecy. The excavators believed that they had found the true relics. After a lengthy deliberation, the authenticity of the relics in the Cathedral of Santiago de Compostela was officially recognized by a papal bull, *Deus Omnipotens,* in 1884.

Twentieth-century excavators led by Sr. Manuel Chamoso Lamas have concentrated on studying the architectural surroundings of the relics and have left the question of their authenticity to the church and to individual conscience. López Ferreiro's reconstruction of the original appearance of the shrine of St. James does not stand the scrutiny of twentieth-century archaeologists although he did excellent work for his time. Modern archaeology provides evidence of a continuity in the history of Santiago de Compostela. The tomb was located in a Roman cemetery beside the principal north-south road through Portugal and Galicia. The graves could date from the first century, and although no specifically Christian symbols have been discovered, the burials are so austere by pagan standards that they may belong to a Christian community. The tomb itself seems to have been a typical large Roman tomb such as those seen along the road near Tarragona in Spain or outside Rome itself. A rectangular edifice two or three stories high and entered from above held the bodies in three chambers in the lowest story. Behind the tomb was a massive Roman wall used by the builders of the Romanesque cathedral as part of the foundations of the transept. Whether this was a retaining wall or even a city wall is debatable. On the south side under part of the present south transept of the cathedral a typical Roman bath was found. Whether this bath belonged to a military camp, a city, or a private estate is impossible to ascertain; however, its presence indicates that a settlement, if not a city, existed on the site of Santiago de Compostela throughout the later Roman period.

The site of the Cathedral of Santiago de Compostela was in more or less continuous use at least from the first century; it did not suffer centuries of abandonment as the legend of the finding of the relics of St. James describes. A large cemetery covering the area occupied by the nave of the present cathedral attests to the successive generations living somewhere near by. With the fall of the Roman Empire the barbarian tribes moved through the Roman lands in waves of migration, each group pushed on in turn by others pouring in from the north and east. Eventually the Suevi moved into Spain and finally to the northwest corner of the peninsula. Over the Roman and perhaps Christian graves in Compostela are layers of Suevi burials. The Suevi graves are, in turn, superseded by medieval burials, and by Asturian churches, Romanesque city walls, and then the foundations for the Romanesque cathedral.

The churches of Alfonso II and Alfonso III can now be reconstructed with considerable accuracy, and they add a new and important dimension to our understanding of the

11

development of early medieval architecture, specifically that style known as "Asturian." The builders of the Asturian churches at Compostela carefully preserved the Roman tomb of the Apostle—the first church was little more than a shed attached to the west wall of the tomb. The church was a simple, single-aisled structure which, in effect, used the tomb of the Apostle as an apse. In the second church, built by the architects of Alphonso III, the sophistication of Asturian architecture, still to be seen in the palace on Mount Naranco or in the splendid Church of San Julián de los Prados near Oviedo, reached its culmination in the largest and most magnificent Asturian building found to date.

The Asturian cathedral was a three-aisled basilica. The tomb of the Apostle still filled the apse, although a passage like a rudimentary ambulatory surrounded the tomb so that the pilgrims could approach the relics. The church could be entered through an open porch or a second door on the south side. On the north side, and evidently connected to the church, was a baptistry with a font and pulpit. The church was probably wooden roofed, as is that of San Julián, although the Asturian builders could construct solid ribbed barrel vaults as they did in the palace at Naranco. The bases of walls and the piers, however, are too slender to support a vault, and the builders may have been loath to attempt a vault on such a large scale. The building was a worthy setting for the relics in the ninth century. The rubble left by Almanzor's destruction, tiny as the fragments are, shows that the building was covered with a veneer of marble and colored stone. The finest marble came from Alexandria, and probably was acquired from Roman buildings in Portugal. After the devastating raids in the tenth century, the church was rebuilt on the same plan, but the rich interior fittings were not replaced. This pre-Romanesque church stood through the eleventh century and was used during the construction of the present cathedral around it. The Asturian building was only removed in 1105 when Pope Urban II dedicated the east end of the new cathedral.

II.
The Road to Santiago de Compostela
and the Medieval Pilgrimage

According to tradition the stars themselves marked the way to St. James, for the Milky Way is a heavenly representation of the road to Santiago de Compostela. Other shrines might rival that of St. James in splendor and renown, but no other pilgrimage had mystique develop around the road itself, making the journey almost rival the importance of the shrine in the mind of the pilgrim. Not only were other important relics located in monasteries and cities along the way, not only did the road pass the sites of Christian heroism fabled in history and legend, but the very road and its bridges were built by such men as Santo Domingo de la Calzada, who were canonized for their pious engineering feats.

Today it seems impossible that Santiago de Compostela could ever have been one of the centers of civilization; however, the spiritual force of the cult of relics drew the thousands of pilgrims to this desolate and isolated spot near the Atlantic coast. The region, called "Finistera," resembles other "land's ends" like Brittany and Cornwall more than the rest of Spain. Yet so great were the throngs of visitors that the word *peregrino* came to refer to pilgrims to the shrine of St. James. The pilgrims to Rome were called *romeros* and those to the Holy Land *palmeros* (Palmers), after the palms which they carried as their symbols, just as the scallop shell was the badge of the *peregrino.*

Around the pilgrimage to St. James grew a body of literature—legends, miracles, folklore, and history—and of music that enriched the cultural life of the entire Western world. Along the road moved masons, carpenters, painters, sculptors, artists, and artisans who created a coherent style which Kingsley Porter called the "pilgrimage style." Down the road came knights, adventurers, and soldiers of fortune ready to fight for a price or an ideal. After completing their pilgrimage, they remained to continue the crusade and the reconquest of Spain. Along the road moved merchants and traders; and the pilgrims themselves carried goods and money to Santiago de Compostela. Towns and monasteries were founded or expanded to provide for the material needs of the travelers. Along the road moved the sick in body and spirit. Beside the road were built some of the great charitable foundations of the Middle Ages, within whose walls medicine, pharmacy, and the biological sciences were being developed to care for the body, in case St. James should not see fit to intervene in the pilgrim's behalf.

The pilgrimage to the shrine of St. James was not simply a peculiar phenomenon of the eleventh and twelfth centuries as many writers on Spanish culture imply. To be sure, the pilgrimage reached the height of its international fame and importance during the twelfth century when throngs of pilgrims made the arduous journey, but the pilgrimage itself was of much earlier foundation and longer duration. As we have seen, in Compostela the pilgrimage was considered to have begun immediately after the identification of the relics of St. James by Bishop Teodomiro and King Alfonso II. Because St. James had been the Apostle to the Iberian peninsula, most of the subsequent political and religious leaders of Spain felt impelled to visit the shrine. Even though the bishop (and later the archbishops) of Santiago might become politically involved with one faction or another, St. James was the patron of the entire peninsula, not just of Galicia, Asturias, León, Castille, Navarre, Aragon, or Catalonia. His shrine was a powerful unifying force throughout the Middle Ages.

Thus in the early Middle Ages Santiago de Compostela joined Rome and Jerusalem as an international pilgrimage center. Jerusalem with the Holy Sepulchre was first in religious importance, and after the organization of the First Crusade in 1095 it was of first military importance as well. Rome had the tomb of St. Peter and was the residence of the pope, who had enormous political as well as spiritual power. Santiago de Compostela, with the tomb of St. James, shared with Jerusalem the threat of Islamic domination; and thus the pilgrimages and concomitant crusades were of primary importance in the political thinking of the church and the Christian rulers.

The pilgrimages to Rome and Jerusalem were, of course, of much greater antiquity than the pilgrimage to Santiago. The tomb of St. Peter and the Sepulchre of Christ were venerated from the earliest Christian period, and the churches were under imperial patronage from the time of the donations of Constantine in the fourth century. That emperor had basilicas erected over the shrines which rivaled in size and splendor the pagan Roman buildings. In contrast to the venerable shrines in Jerusalem and Rome, the tomb and church of St. James at first would have appeared very humble indeed if it were not for the talent of the monastic propagandists. The large numbers of pilgrims to Spain did not arise out of spontaneous piety alone but from very skillful organization on the part of the church. Even the archbishop of Santiago, Gelmírez, traveled through France and Italy in the early twelfth century preaching the pilgrimage to his cathedral.

To a large extent the monks of the Congregation of Cluny stimulated and organized the pilgrimage. Cluny was founded in 910 in Burgundy as a reform movement within the Benedictine order. Favored by a secure geographical location in the age of Islamic and Viking invasions and led by the brilliant and dynamic abbots, the Cluniacs flourished and soon became one of the leading intellectual and spiritual forces in the early Middle Ages. This spiritual leadership evolved into political and economic power as well, until by the twelfth century the Congregation had become a religious, political, and economic empire of international scope. The fortunes of Christian Spain were of great concern to the monks. King Alfonso VI was one of the major contributors to the building of the new monastic church at Cluny; he had French wives, his two daughters married Burgundian nobles, and his confessor was a monk of Cluny. Cluniac and Augustinian monks dominated the religious life of Alfonso's realm. Powerful as Cluny was, however, it was not alone in its sponsorship of the pilgrimage to Compostela. Augustinians, Hospitalers and other orders also established houses along the Road.

The Pilgrimage Road (or the "French Road" as it was often called) described by Aymery Picaud in his *Pilgrims' Guide* did not become popular until the end of the eleventh century. The earliest routes followed the northern coast of the peninsula, but as soon as the crusade against the Moors made such a change feasible, the pilgrims followed inland roads to avoid the constant threat of attacks by pirates, not the least of whom were the Vikings who harried the north coast of Spain throughout the ninth and tenth centuries.

Pilgrims as well as pirates used the sea routes to Compostela, landing at Padrón or La Coruña. Naturally these sea routes were favored throughout the Middle Ages by English and Scandinavian pilgrims who were accustomed to travel by ship. These seafaring pilgrims often also planned to visit Rome or the Holy Land. Such a pilgrim was Sigurd, King of the Isles, younger son of King Magnus Barefoot of Norway, and ultimately king of Norway himself. His travels are not unusual. Sigurd and his men sailed for the Holy Land in sixty ships in the fall of 1108 or 1109. After stays in England and France they wintered the second year in Galicia. When supplies ran low and the local count (probably the Count of Traba) broke his promise to sell them food, the Norse pilgrims attacked the count's castle and took not only food but everything else as well. The next spring they departed, visiting first Portugal (where they fought five battles against the Moors) and then Roger, the Norman king of Sicily. The pilgrims participated in the siege of Sideon in Palestine, visited Byzantium where Sigurd was received by the emperor, and then returned home in 1111 or 1112. It is easy to understand why such pilgrims, although nominally Christian, might be considered by the native population to be marauders. When ten to twelve thousand pilgrims from northern Europe in a fleet of fifty ships landed at La Coruña at Easter time in 1189, they were forced to leave without completing their pilgrimage by the frightened townspeople, who doubted their purely religious intentions (it was rumored that they planned to steal the head of the Apostle).

By the twelfth century the land route of the pilgrims across northern Spain was well established. The pilgrims traveled through France on one of four major roads, three of which joined to cross the Pyrenees at Roncesvalles. Pilgrims from Italy and Provence might enter Spain on the

Mediterranean coast, travel through Catalonia, and visit the shrine at Montserrat and later the Church of Our Lady of the Pillar at Zaragoza. Pilgrims intent on visiting all the great shrines of Christendom might include this Catalan pilgrimage on the way to or from Rome and the Holy Land. Other variations in the itinerary included important shrines such as the monastery of Santo Domingo de Silos south of the road near Burgos. The most important detour led north from León to Oviedo where the *Cámara Santa* of the cathedral contained the most precious collection of relics to be found in Spain. (An Asturian proverb said that to visit Santiago de Compostela and not Oviedo was to pay homage to the servant and not the master.)

In spite of all these variations the phrase "pilgrimage road" conjures up the image of the route described in the *Pilgrims' Guide.* The guide, properly called the *Liber Sancti Jacobi,* was probably compiled under the direction of Aymery Picaud of Parthenay, the chancellor of Pope Calixtus. It is found in *Codex Calixtinus* which is composed of five books: *The Offices of the Church of Santiago de Compostela, The Miracles of St. James, The Life and Translation of St. James, The Expedition of Charlemagne to Spain,* and *The Pilgrims' Guide.* The Codex was attributed to Pope Calixtus II, but it was neither written nor compiled by him. The authors wanted to give the maximum authority to their work, and thus throughout the five books they attributed various sections to the most illustrious man of the time. Of special interest to the cultural historian is the rich collection of music and literature, including the exploits of Charlemagne in Spain and the *Pilgrims' Guide.*

Although Aymery Picaud may not have actually written the *Guide,* someone from Poitou or Saintonge composed it in the second quarter of the twelfth century. Unlike most accounts of pilgrimages which are simple itineraries, the *Guide* provided valuable information for the trip, a description of the route and cities, the character of countries and people, religious highlights and relics to be visited, and such practical matters as hospitals, the quality of food and water, and a brief vocabulary guide to the Basque language. It also has a detailed description of the city and Cathedral of Santiago de Compostela. In short, it is one of the most interesting documents to survive from the twelfth century.

The first six chapters of the *Guide* are concerned with the route. Naturally for the successful completion of an international journey, the lives and fortunes of the travelers had to be relatively secure. A regular chain of monastic houses was established throughout France and northern Spain; thus the pilgrims not only were urged to travel but also were guided and cared for along the way. The road was kept in repair, bridges were built, and when necessary ferries were operated. At key spots stood hospitals. The trip from the Pyrenees to Compostela was planned in thirteen stages with hostels spaced at intervals of a day's journey and more extensive facilities available at large cities and major shrines.

"There are four roads leading to Santiago which unite in a single road at Puente la Reina, in Spanish territory. One goes through St. Gilles, Montpellier, Toulouse, and Somport; another passes Notre Dame du Puy, Ste. Foy de Conques and St. Pierre de Moissac; another passes Ste. Marie Madeleine de Vézelay, St. Léonard in the Limousin, and the city of Perigueux; still another passes through St. Martin de Tours, St. Hilarie de Poitiers, St. Jean d'Angély, St. Eutrope de Saintes, and the city of Bordeaux.

"The roads by way of Ste. Foy, St. Léonard, and St.

Martin meet at Ostabat, and after having crossed the pass at Cize, join the road which went by way of Somport at Puente la Reina; from there only one road leads to Santiago."

Chapter two lists the stages of the road, and chapter three, the cities (the list of cities is included here with overnight stops italicized).

"From Somport to Puente la Reina here are the cities which one finds on the route to Santiago: Borce is first, at the foot of the mountain on the Gascon side; then after having climbed the crest of the mountain one finds the hospital of Ste. Christine; then Canfranc; *Jaca*; then Ostruit; Tiermas, where there are some royal baths in which the waters are always hot; then *Monreal*; finally one reaches *Puente la Reina.*

"From the pass of Cize, here are the most important cities which one finds on the road of St. James to the basilica of Galicia: first at the foot of the mountain of Cize, on the Gascon side, there is the city of St. Michel; then after having crossed the crest of the mountain, one reaches the hospital of Roland, then the city of Roncesvalles; one finds next *Viscarret*; then Larrasoaña; then the city of *Pamplona*; then Puenta la Reina; then *Estella* where the bread is good, the wine excellent, and the meat and fish abundant and every delicacy is available. [Horses are recommended for this and the following stage in chapter two.]

"One passes then by Los Arcos, Logroño, Villaroya; then one finds the city of *Nájera,* Santo Domingo de la Calzada, Redecilla, Belorado, Villafranca, the forest of Oca, Atapuerca, the city of *Burgos,* Tardajos, Hornillos del Camino, Castrogeriz, the bridge of Itero, *Frómista;* Carrión de los Condes which is an industrious and prosperous city rich in bread, in wine, in meat, and in all kinds of things; then there is *Sahagún* where prosperity reigns; then a plain where it is said that the lances of victorious warriors, planted for the glory of God, were still visible in the greenish field.

"Then there is Mansilla and the city of *León,* residence of the king and the court, filled with all kinds of pleasures. Then there is Hospital de Orbigo; then the city of Astorga; then *Rabanal del Camino,* called the captive; then Puerto Irago, Molinaseca, then Ponferrada, Cacabelos, *Villafranca* at the mouth of the Valcarde; then Castro Sarracín, Villaus, the slope of the mountain Cebrero and the hospital at the summit of the mountain; then Linares, the *Triacastela* at the foot of the mountains in Galicia. It is there that the pilgrims get a block of limestone to carry with them to Castañola to make lime for mortar which is used in the construction of the Apostle's basilica. Then there is the city of San Miguel, Barbardelo, then the bridge over the Miño (Puertomarin) then Sala Regina, *Palas de Rey,* Leboreiro, then Santiago de Boente, Castañola, Vilanova, Ferreiros; finally *Compostela,* the very excellent city of the Apostle, filled with all delights. There the precious body of St. James is kept, and the city is known as the most fortunate and noble in Spain.

"And if I have enumerated rapidly the cities and stages, it is so that the pilgrims who leave for Santiago will be informed in advance and can plan ahead for the trip." (Book V, chapter III)

Chapter six includes both practical advice and travelers' tales along with geographical notes beginning with the rivers.

"Here are the rivers that one encounters between the

passes of Cize and Somport and Santiago: from Somport there descends a healthful river by the name of Aragón which irrigates Spain; from the port of Cize flows a healthy river which many call the Runa and which passes Pamplona. At Puente la Reina the Arga and the Runa meet; in a place called Lorce towards the east flows a river called the salty stream; there be careful not to water your horse for this river is deadly. On its banks when we were going to Santiago we found two Navarrese seated sharpening their knives: they made a practice of skinning the mounts of the pilgrims who drank this water and died. To our question they replied with a lie saying that this water was good and drinkable; we watered our horses, and at once two of them died and these people flayed them on the field.

"At Estella flows the river Ega whose water is sweet, healthy, and excellent; the city which one calls Los Arcos is cut by a ravine with a stream where the water is deadly; and after Los Arcos, near the first hospice, that is between Los Arcos and this hospice, flows a river which is fatal to horses and to men who drink from it. After a village called Turres, in Navarrese territory flows a river which kills horses and men who drink the water. From there to a village called Covas flows a stream of unhealthy water.

"At Logroño a large river named the Ebro passes. In it the water is good, and it abounds with fish. All the rivers one finds from Estella to Logroño have water dangerous for men and horses to drink, and the fish are poisonous to those who eat them. There is a fish which is commonly called *barbo* or which the Poitevins call *alosam* and the Italian *clipiam* or *ealor*. Do not eat fish in Spain, or in Galicia, for undoubtedly you will die shortly afterwards, or at least you will become ill. If someone should by chance eat it and not fall sick, he is simply much healthier than others or, more likely, he has become acclimated by a long stay in the country. All the fish, beef and pork in all of Spain and Galicia make foreigners sick.

[Here follows a list of ten rivers with sweet and healthy drinking water.]

"If I have described these rivers, it is in order that the pilgrims going to St. Santiago should be careful not to drink unhealthy water and should be able to choose those rivers which are good for them and their mounts." (Book V, chapter VI)

———

The road builders in Spain made use of Roman roads whenever they could. (The Romans had built a road linking Tarragona and La Coruña in order to exploit the mines in the province of León and to facilitate military maneuvers and trading operations.) The Roman roads and bridges were excellently built and have remained in use, although often in disrepair, right to the present century. The maintenance of these roads was the responsibility of the local lord and was looked on as a Christian duty which conferred considerable spiritual benefits. When Roman roads were not available, roads and bridges had to be constructed. So important and difficult was this work and such an act of charity was it considered to be that these early highway engineers are mentioned by name in the *Guide.*

———

"Here are the names of some builders who in the time of Diego [Gelmírez], Alfonso [VII], emperor of Spain and Galicia, and Pope Calixtus who rebuilt the road of St. James from Rabanal to the bridge over the Miño, for the love of God and St. James, before the year 1120, during the reigns of Alfonso [I], king of Aragón and of Louis [VI] the Fat, king of France: Andreas, Rotgerius, Alvitus, Fortus, Arnaldus, Stephanus, and Petrus who built the bridge over the Miño destroyed by Queen Urraca.

"May the souls of these men and those of their helpers rest in eternal peace." (Book V, chapter V)

———————

The bridges still standing attest to the excellence of Petrus' and other medieval stone masons' technique. The rivers were crossed by the same great barrel vaults of stone voussoirs that were used to vault the naves of the finest churches. The stone was cut with great care, and each block fitted accurately into its place in order that as little mortar as possible might be used. A chapel often was placed at one side, or in the center of the bridge, and a cell or hospice of a monk who tended the bridge stood beside it. Only a solid stone bridge could resist the elements, especially the possibility of flooding, and function in the essential transportation and communication system tying Santiago de Compostela with the rest of the Christian world. The pilgrimage and with it the economic and political life of the country were dependent on the roads.

Without a well-kept road system the city of Santiago de Compostela could not have existed as an international intellectual and cultural center. When the transportation and communication system was disrupted, the city declined into a provincial capital. Such is the possible fate of any city. The very ferment which is the heart of a city is not self-producing, but depends on its hinterland, and thus on its transportation and communication system for its economic and intellectual life. The builder monk, Santo Domingo de la Calzada deserved his fame. People in the twelfth century sensed the vital role he and other builders played in the viability of Santiago de Compostela.

Closely linked to the problem of public transportation was (then as now) the problem of public safety. The traveler to Santiago de Compostela, from the poorest penitent to the richest lord, required protection from the human hazards of an already arduous journey. The pilgrim to Santiago de Compostela was accorded special privileges of free passage through territories and, in effect, a safe conduct. The treatment to be accorded the pilgrim is set forth in the last book of the *Pilgrims' Guide.*

"The pilgrims, be they poor or rich, who come to Santiago or who want to go there ought to be received with charity and regard by all; for whosoever receives them and gives them shelter has given shelter not only to St. James but to our Lord himself as it was said in the Gospel, *'Qui vos recipit me recipit.'* Many are those who have incurred the wrath of God because they have not taken in the pilgrims of St. James or the beggars.

"At Nantua, which is a town situated between Geneva and Lyon, a cloth merchant refused bread to a pilgrim of Santiago who asked him for it; suddenly he saw his linen fall down torn apart through the middle. At Vilanova a poor pilgrim to Compostela asked alms for the love of God and the blessed James from a woman who had placed bread under hot ashes. She told him she had no bread, to which the pilgrim responded, 'I hope to heaven your bread changes to stone.' The pilgrim left the house and continued his journey, and when that woman went to the ashes to get her bread, she found in its place only a round stone. With a contrite heart she went out to look for the pilgrim, but she did not find him.

"At Poitiers two courageous but destitute French pilgrims returning from Santiago came to the house of Jean

Gautier near St. Porchaire and asked alms for the love of St. James, but they were given none. Finally at the most recently built house on that street near the basilica of St. Porchaire, they were taken in by a poor man. Then by divine vengeance, that very night, a violent fire started and rapidly destroyed the entire street, beginning with the house where the pilgrims had first asked for hospitality and continuing up to the one where they were taken in. Almost a thousand houses were destroyed, but that in which the servants of God had been received was saved by His Grace.

"This is why everyone ought to know that, rich or poor, the pilgrims to Santiago are entitled to hospitality and a kind reception." (Book V, chapter XI)

In spite of such strictures the pilgrim was often robbed or mistreated by bandits or unscrupulous local residents. Those who collected turnpike fees are singled out for special condemnation in the sermons of the *Codex Calixtinus.*

"And what shall we say of those who exact tribute from the pilgrims to Santiago? The Collectors at the turnpikes of Ostabat, of San Juan, and of San Miguel at the foot of pass of Cize are to be condemned above all. Words cannot describe the injuries they have done pilgrims. Seldom does one pass by without being exploited by them." (Sermon by Pope Calixtus, Feast of the Translation of St. James, Book I, chapter XVII)

Informally at first, a few knights took up the duty of protecting travelers through their lands. By the twelfth century this sporadic protection was extended along the entire road, and a group of knights were organized into the Order of Santiago. (The order became one of the most important noble orders in Europe.) In 1167, King Fernando II approved the Order of the Knights of Santiago of the Sword *(Caballeros de Santiago de la Espada)* when he was in the city of Alcantara. They had their first headquarters in Cáceres and were often called the Knights of Cáceres. The archbishop of Compostela especially favored these knights and made their leader an honorary canon of the cathedral. The order established a new headquarters in León and built the commandery and hospice of San Marco. The Rule of the Order, as confirmed in Rome, established a single head, or *maestre,* and three commanders to meet in an annual chapter meeting. Their original duties were to fight the Moors, not for worldly glory or joy in bloodshed but to protect Christians and to convert the Moors to Christianity.

A papal bull confirmed the foundation July 5, 1175. The duties of the knights were extended from fighting the Moors to guarding the roads and travelers, providing hospitality for pilgrims, and, of course, serving the king. The thirteen original knights were commemorated even when the order grew very large by electing thirteen commanders as a council to the *maestre.* Two other knightly orders were founded in the twelfth century and are often confused with the Knights of Santiago: the Order of Alcantara and the Order of Calatrava. (The Knights of Santiago did not take part in the siege of Alcantara, nor did they hold the citadel; however, one of their commanders held it for a time as a personal fief. When Alcantara was retaken by Alfonso IX in 1214, he gave it to the Order of Calatrava. The Order of Alcantara originated at San Julian de Pereiro in Portugal.) In any event, the traveler to Santiago de Compostela could hope for some protection and, when he reached León, a hospital and hostel where he could rest in safety before crossing the mountains into Galicia.

The Knights of Santiago could not protect the traveler from the evils of the innkeepers. The pilgrim had to rely on his wits and his patron saint. The tales of the intervention of St. James on behalf of a pilgrim were popular during the twelfth century and appear in painting and sculpture as well as in literature. A hanging boy or a crowing cock carved on the portal of a church reminded the pilgrims of the family who were traveling to Santiago de Compostela: one night at an inn the son rejected the advances of a girl, who in revenge slipped two silver cups into his pack. As the pilgrims were about to depart in the morning, the girl denounced the boy to the innkeeper. In spite of his protests of innocence he was hanged, and his parents continued their pilgrimage to Santiago de Compostela. On their return they found their son still alive on the scaffold. He told them that St. James himself had supported and sustained him. The parents rushed to the village demanding their son's release and pardon; however, neither the innkeeper nor the lord would believe them. The lord said it was as likely that the boy was alive as it was that the cock, and he pointed to the roast fowl on the table, should stand up and crow. Whereupon the roasted cock stood up on the platter and crowed three times. Needless to say, after such a sign, the boy—alive, healthy, and vindicated—was cut down from the scaffold, and the happy pilgrims went on their way home. Incidentally, a century later, Mary replaced St. James in this story; in the Gothic period she gradually supplanted many saints in the popular imagination.

The road to Compostela was filled with hazards, and St. James could not be relied on to provide an endless succession of miracles. Today we are accustomed to travel with ease, and with our English literary heritage, we think of pilgrimages in terms of Chaucer's *Canterbury Tales.* We must remember that the trip from London to Canterbury in the fourteenth century was a pleasure outing compared with the trip from Vézelay or St. Gilles to Santiago de Compostela in the twelfth. The most vivid impression of the trip may be gained from chapter seven of the *Pilgrims' Guide,* that is, the description of the countries and people to be encountered by the pilgrim traveling from southwestern France to Compostela. The author of this chapter must have written from personal experience, for he brings the journey to Santiago and some of the people of Spain alive to us.

"Going to Santiago by way of Toulouse, after having first crossed the Garonne, one arrives in Gascony, and thereafter having climbed the peak of Somport, Aragón, the Navarre, and so on. But if one takes the route by way of the pass of Cize, after Tours one finds oneself in Poitou, which is a fertile, excellent, happy land. The Poitevins are vigorous people and good warriors, skillful in the use of the bows, arrows, and lances, courageous in the front of battle, very fast in races, elegant in their manner of dress, beautiful, spiritual, very generous and hospitable. [Chauvinism is clearly not a modern development.] Then one enters Saintonge; from there after having crossed an arm of the sea and the Garonne one arrives in the Bordelais where the wine is excellent, the fish abundant but the language crude. . . . Then three tiring days are needed to cross the region of Landes. This is a desolate country lacking everything. . . . If by chance you cross Landes in summer take something to protect your face from the enormous flies that fly around everywhere. . . . And if you don't watch your feet carefully you will sink rapidly up to the knees in the encroaching sea sand.

"After having crossed this country, one comes to Gascony, rich in white bread and excellent red wine; it is covered with woods, meadows, streams, and pure springs. The Gascons are frivolous, braggards, mockers, debauchers, drunkards, gluttons, badly dressed, and careless with money; however, they are well-trained warriors and remarkable for their hospitality to the poor. Seated around a fire, they usually eat without a table and all drink from the same goblet. They eat a lot, drink to the dregs, and are badly dressed; they think nothing of all sleeping together on a thin pallet of straw, the servants along with the master and mistress.

"On leaving that country the road to St. James crosses two rivers. . . . It is impossible to cross them except in a boat. Curses on Ferrymen. Actually each of the streams is narrow. The people are, however, accustomed to take a coin from each man that must cross to the other side whether he be poor or rich, and for a horse they forcibly extort four coins. Their boat is small, made from a single tree trunk, making it difficult to carry horses. Also when one gets on, one must be very careful not to get on with many passengers, for if the boat is too loaded it will sink.

"More than once after having received their money, the ferrymen have loaded on such a large troop of pilgrims that the boat capsized, and the pilgrims drowned; and then the evil boatmen rejoiced and robbed the dead.

"Surrounding the pass of Cize is the Basque territory. . . . This country has a barbarous language, and is wooded, mountainous, and lacks bread, wine, and food of all kinds; however, one finds some compensation in the apples, cider, and milk.

"This country is inhabited by evil people . . . the people frankly should be sent to the Devil. They actually surround the pilgrims with two or three sticks to extort by force an unjust tribute. And if some traveler refuses to yield to their demands and to give them money, they beat him with the sticks, take the tax from him, injure him, and strip him. . . . The ferocity of their faces and appearance and their barbarous speech terrifies everyone who sees them. . . .

[Here follows a demand for excommunication.]

"In the Basque country, the route of Santiago climbs a remarkable mountain called the pass of Cize . . . this mountain is so high that it seems to touch the sky; he who climbs it could believe he would be able to touch the sky with his own hand. . . . On the summit of this mountain is a place named the Cross of Charles *(Crux Karoli)* because it was here that Charlemagne and his army . . . cleared a passage on the way to Spain and that he first erected a cross and knelt before it, and turning towards Galicia he addressed a prayer to God and St. James. Thus, when they arrive here, the pilgrims usually kneel and pray, turning toward the country of St. James, and each places his cross like a standard. One can find almost a thousand crosses there. . . . It is on this mountain, before Christianity was spread widely in Spain, that the impious Navarrese and the Basques were accustomed not only to strip the pilgrims going to Santiago but also to ride them like asses and to kill some of them. Near this mountain toward the north is a valley called Charles's Valley *(Vallis Karoli)* in which Charlemagne took refuge with his army after the warriors had been killed at Roncesvalles. It is through this valley that the pilgrims pass when they do not want to climb the mountain.

"On the descending slope one finds the hospice and the church with the rock which that superhuman hero, Roland, split from the top to bottom through the middle with a triple blow of his sword. Next one comes to Roncesvalles, the site of the great battle in which King Marsile, Roland, Oliver, and 40,000 other Christian and Moorish warriors died. After this valley, one enters Navarre. . . .

"The Navarrese wear short black tunics which come

only to their knees like the Scots; they wear shoes which they call *lavarcas* made of raw leather still covered with hair, which they attach around their feet with cords but which cover only the bottom of the foot, leaving the top bare. They wear elbow-length cloaks of dark-colored fringed wool, like a hood, which they call *saias*. These people are poorly dressed and eat and drink badly. At home the Navarrese family—servants and master, maids and mistress—all eat food mixed together in a single dish. They eat with their hands without spoons, and they drink from the same goblet. Watching them eat reminds one of dogs or pigs feeding gluttonously. Hearing them speak reminds one of barking dogs. Their language is completely barbarous. . . . [Here follow examples of words.]

"This is a barbarous people, different from all people, and both through custom and race, filled with trickery, black in color, heavy in face, debauched, perverse, perfidious, disloyal, corrupt, voluptuous, drunken, expert in all violences, ferocious and savage, dishonest and false, impious and crude, cruel and quarrelsome, incapable of all good feeling, inclined to every vice and iniquity. These people resemble the Getes and the Moors in their malice and in every sort of enmity to our people of France. For only a sou the Navarrese or the Basques would kill a Frenchman, if they could. . . .

[The Basque and Navarrese are further maligned by the writer before he continues his description of the country.]

"After this country one travels through the forest of Oca toward Burgos, and the land of Spain that is the country of Castile. This country is filled with riches, gold and silver, fodder and vigorous horses; and bread, wine, meat, fish, milk, and honey abound; however, it lacks wood, and is inhabited by tricky, vicious people.

"Then one comes to Galicia, after crossing León and

the mountains Irago and Cebrero. Here the countryside is wooded, crossed by rivers, well provided with meadows and excellent grassy plots. The fruits are good and the springs are clear, but cities, villages, and cultivated fields are rare. Wheat bread and wine are scarce, but one finds lots of rye bread and cider, cattle and horses, milk and honey, enormous ocean fish and small fish. Also gold, silver, fine fabrics, wild animal furs, and other riches abound there, as well as sumptuous Moorish treasures.

"Among all the civilized people of Spain the people of Galicia are most like our race, the French, in their habits, but they are, it is said, inclined to be hot-tempered and litigious." (Book V, chapter VII)

Thus the author of the *Guide* assures the traveler of an easier journey and better treatment as he approaches his destination. After all, the pilgrim needed to be warned of the hazards but not discouraged from making his trip.

III.
The Goal of the Pilgrimage:
The City and the Cathedral

As he reached the crest of the last low mountain on the French road, the foot-weary or saddle-sore pilgrim saw Santiago de Compostela before him, and he stopped there at Monte del Gozo to offer prayers of joy and thanksgiving. The city itself was located on a low hill formed by the valleys of two small rivers, the Sar and the Sarela. Compostela was dominated by its huge fortified cathedral and protected by walls and towers, a necessary precaution against pirates, Moors, and the local noblemen who often behaved like bandits. To the west outside the gates lay the ancient *castro* or fortified hill, now crowned by a church built by the Archbishop Gelmírez. It was here that on more than one occasion besieging armies assembled.

Although the walls of Santiago de Compostela are no longer standing, their location and the subsequent expansion of the city is reflected in the present plan of the city. The eleventh-century walls enclosed a relatively small rectangular area east and south of the cathedral. They ran along the present streets of the Azabachería, Preguntorio, Gelmírez, and the Obradorio. They did not include the most defensible areas; however, this lack of military foresight can be explained by the religious requirements of the site. Recent excavations show that the major north-south Roman road ran approximately along the south side of the present cloister, and that a city or camp of some size was located east of the site of the present cathedral. As we have seen in Chapter I, a wall and a bath were uncovered in the foundations of the south transept, and the early cemetery and tomb were aligned with these Roman structures. Thus when a church was built including the tomb as its sanctuary, the site of that church—and therefore of the religious community—could not be selected with an eye either to convenience or defensibility. Both the ancient *castro* and the high point in the terrain (the present Plaza de San Roque) were originally outside the city walls.

The city was enlarged twice during the Romanesque period, once southward in the mid-eleventh century and again in the early twelfth century. A section of the eleventh-century wall and a tower were found under three western bays of the nave of the cathedral. The wall is 1.80 meters thick, and the tower 7.45 meters square. This tower had a facing of fine ashlar masonry and a rubble-and-mortar fill, and it was strengthened at the base with additional courses of stone. Sections of the twelfth-century wall were still standing and indicated in an 1837 military plan. The location of these walls is marked by the broad avenue surrounding the old city. Santiago is described in the *Pilgrims' Guide:*

"Between the two rivers, one of which is called the Sar and the other the Sarela, rises the city of Compostella; the Sar is to the east between Monte del Gozo [San Marcos] and the city; the Sarela is to the west. The city has seven gates or entrances. The first gate is called *porta Francigena;* the second, *porta Penne;* the third, *porta de Subfratribus;* the fourth, *porta de Sancto Peregrino;* the fifth, *porta de*

Falgueriis leading to Padrón; the sixth, *porta de Susannis;* the seventh, *porta de Macerellis* where the precious Bacchus [wine] enters the city." (Codex Calixtinus, Book V, chapter IX)

———————————

The *porta Francigena* is today the *Puerta del Camino,* a reference to the pilgrimage road. The second, *porta Penne,* is on the north side of the city and refers to the Penna, or mountain peaks of the north. The third, *porta Subfratribus,* to the east, is now the *Puerta de San Martin* and took its name from the monastic hospice located near it. The fourth gate, *Sancto Peregrino,* is now the *Puerta de la Trinidad.* The fifth, *Falgueriis,* is the *Puerta Fajera,* the square at the elegant public gardens and the *Paseo de la Herradura;* the sixth, the *porta de Susannis,* is the busy little crossroads, *la Mamoa,* in the heart of the old city. The seventh, *porta de Macerellis,* is the only gate which is still even partly standing, and is known as the *Arco de Mazarelos* in the *Plaza del Instituto.* Since this square was formerly called the old market place and the *Guide* refers to the wine's coming there, this gate was evidently the principal tradesmen's entrance to the city.

From afar Santiago de Compostela must have looked very much like Avila today. Avila is oval in shape with the cathedral at one side, its apse forming one tower in the wall. The impression is that of a castle and keep with the city wall forming a curtain wall reinforced by battlemented towers of solid masonry. Gates had double towers and massive wooden doors reinforced with iron. In Santiago de Compostela, after the civil disorders of 1116–17, the cathedral was fortified and formed the strong point of the city, although unlike the cathedral of Avila it was not part of the walls.

Santiago de Compostela was fancifully likened to the

shape of the scallop shell of St. James, and although the form is certainly accidental, Compostela had a roughly convex, shell-like shape caused by the rising hill and location of the major streets running its length. The Rua del Villar and the Calle del Franco (named for D. Alonso de Fonseca, *el franco*) are still the major arteries leading to the cathedral from the *Puerta Fajera* and the *Puerta de la Mamoa.* The French pilgrims following the *Pilgrims' Guide,* however, approached the city from the northeast. They passed a leprosarium, crossed the river, traversed a small grove of trees, climbed the low hill, and entered the city through the *Puerta Francigena.* They progressed toward the cathedral by the Via Francigena, the only major east-west street, and so on to the Paraiso, or square, in front of the north transept of the cathedral. The Paraiso of the cathedral was the commercial center of the town. To walk this route today one goes from the *Puerta del Camino,* climbs the hill by way of *Las Casas Reales, Plaza de Cervantes,* down the *Azabachería* to the *Plaza de la Immaculada,* and finally the north side of the cathedral.

The Paraiso was a large, open, paved square, bordered by the north transept portal of the cathedral on its south side, the archbishop's palace on the west, a hospital for pilgrims on the northwest corner, the Church and monastery of St. Martin on the north, and the Church of St. Mary (the Corticela) and the Church and monastery of St. Pelayo as well as houses and commercial buildings on the east. In the square was a very remarkable fountain, surely one of the finest erected in the twelfth century. The pilgrims and citizens had suffered from the lack of water until an aqueduct was constructed which brought fresh water in from northeast of the city. Inside the city an underground channel divided, with one channel carrying the water to the monastery of St. Martin and the other to the public fountain. This huge fountain of granite and bronze was erected by Bernardo, the treasurer of the cathedral. The basin may still be seen in the cloister of the cathedral although the fountain was dismantled in the fifteenth century. The fountain and paraiso are described in the *Pilgrims' Guide:*

"When we French want to go into the Basilica of the Apostle, we enter on the north side. In front of the portal and by the roadside is the hospice of poor pilgrims to Santiago; and then farther along the road one finds a square which one reaches by going down nine steps. At the foot of the steps is an admirable fountain which is without parallel in the entire world; this fountain rests on a base of three large stone steps which supports a round, concave, shell-like stone basin which is so large that it seems to me that fifteen men could bathe in it with ease. From its center rises a column of bronze larger at the base, composed of seven flat panels, of a well-proportioned height, and from whose summit four lions project, from whose mouths fall four jets of water for the use of the pilgrims to Santiago and the citizens of the city; and these streams after having left the jaws of the lions, fall into the basin which surrounds them and from there the water flows through an opening in the basin and disappears underground. Thus one is not able to see from whence the water comes nor where it goes. Furthermore, this water is sweet, nutritious, healthy, clear, excellent, warm in winter and cool in summer. On the column the following inscription is engraved in two lines all the way round under the feet of the lions: 'I, Bernardo, treasurer of Santiago, have brought this water here and erected this monument for the good of my soul and the souls of my parents, era 1160, III Ides of April [that is, April 11, 1122].'

"Beyond the fountain one finds the paraiso or square as we have noted, paved with stone, where the pilgrims are sold the scallop shells which are the badges of St. James and also wineskins, shoes, deerskin satchels, purses, straps, belts, and all sorts of medicinal herbs, and other drugs and many other things. The money-changers, the inn-keepers, and other merchants are also in the Via Francigena. The square is a stone's throw in each direction." (Book V, chapter IX)

The city must have seemed more like a commercial than a religious center. The streets were lined with shops, taverns, and hospices catering to the pilgrims' needs, and if we are to believe the sermon included in Book Two of the Codex Calixtinus, the streets were fraught with dangers for the unwary foreigner. Pope Calixtus' description of the inn-keepers of Santiago de Compostela in the twelfth century could be repeated in every age and in every place afflicted by a "tourist invasion." During the spring and fall, the periods of maximum influx of pilgrims, Santiago de Compostela must have been a very exciting and crowded cosmopolitan center.

Only the large monastic and public establishments could begin to house the thousands who flocked to the shrine, for the private houses and hostels were small. Private houses in Santiago de Compostela in the twelfth century were generally two or three stories high. Upper floors of rather light materials (wood, wattle and daub) were raised over a more solid ground floor, often built of stone. On the ground floor were stables and offices, shops and workrooms. In the case of shops, the shutters which covered their openings at night formed tables for display of goods during the day. Over the commercial or industrial first floor were the living quarters of the family. Yet another floor might rise over that and provide additional sleeping or storage space, including space to rent to pilgrims. An interesting commentary on domestic architecture is found in the story of Archbishop Gelmírez' escape in the civil uprising of 1117 (see Chapter V). So light was the construction of the houses that Gelmírez was able to travel rapidly through the city, from the monastery of St. Martin to the home of one of his supporters, without entering the streets by moving from house to house, breaking through the common walls. No wonder a fire could quickly destroy an entire district of a medieval city.

The monasteries and convents of Compostela also provided as much or more housing than the private dwellings. In Santiago de Compostela every monastic order had an establishment, and in this city the monastic contributions to social welfare were particularly important. The monks provided education, medical treatment and care for indigents, and hospices for pilgrims. The church was naturally the major building in a monastery, and the cloister, when possible, was placed on the southern, warmer side of the church. The cloister formed a center square much like the public square of a city. (Cloisters were built both in monasteries and in the churches such as the Cathedral of Santiago in which the clergy was organized in a semimonastic community.) Church, chapter house, dormitory, refectory, and library were joined by the cloister walks. Usually the chapter house stood at the east, and over it was a dormitory with stairs leading directly into the church for night services. Refectory, kitchen, and often the library were on the south side of the cloister. Wine cellars and other essential rooms were often on the west. Workshops and gardens, fish ponds, farms, and stables, made the monastery a self-sufficient economic unit. Medieval monasteries were not places of quiet retreat, although they were first and foremost religious centers. The monastery was the social service and welfare center of the Middle Ages, as well as the school, the hotel, the concert hall, and theater; the manufacturing center for the production of metal, jeweled, enameled, and ivory objects; the most important if not the only publishing house, the research institute, and the medical center. It was a city in itself, bustling with activity. All the orders had establishments along the pilgrimage road to provide for the welfare of the pilgrims, not entirely charitable service since the pilgrims contributed a great deal of money to the coffers in the form of pious donations and payments for supplies, transportation, equipment, and badges and souvenirs.

The monastic buildings other than the church and cloister—that is, the hospitals and hospices, and in the twelfth century the private quarters of the monks as well—were usually simple, barnlike buildings. The most elaborate were two-story masonry structures, and the simplest had wooden frames, wattle-and-daub walls, and timber roofs. In hospices a single large room provided shelter for all. A twelfth-century capital in San Gil de Luna, province of Zaragoza, shows people sleeping at an inn wrapped in their cloaks and lying in rows like sausages. Sanitary facilities included latrines, constructed whenever possible over rivers.

The hospitals for sick or destitute pilgrims in Santiago de Compostela were more imposing than most others in the twelfth century, although they were rivaled in size and number by the establishments all along the pilgrimage road. The principal hospital was built between the archbishop's palace and the monastery of St. Martin. In the medieval hospital large halls opened on a chapel, for miracles played a more important role than medicine. Spain was profiting from Moorish and Jewish medical knowledge; however, the great doctors of Córdoba usually had to be consulted secretly, since their skill was linked to the powers of darkness. A specialized medical institution was the leprosarium. An outbreak of leprosy spread like a plague over Europe in the twelfth century. Houses dedicated to St. Lazarus were established in the outskirts of Santiago and other cities to care for the unfortunate victims who otherwise were forced to live on alms in isolated colonies. One of the noteworthy early charitable foundations in Santiago de Compostela was the monastery and hospital of St. Lazarus, founded as a co-operative project of the church and private persons.

The most important secular building in Santiago was the palace of the Archbishop. Although rebuilt in the thirteenth century, the essential structure remains, and the palace, as the finest house surviving from the period, gives us an idea of the splendor of the court in the twelfth century. The building has a T-shaped plan in which the cross bar joins the northwest tower of the cathedral, continuing the line of the façade, and the upright lies parallel to the nave. An open patio is left between palace and cathedral, and a private garden extends east toward the Paraiso. The ground floor of the palace contains an elegant room divided into two aisles by a row of columns with foliate capitals. A door at each end opens into a passage. This room provided quarters for guards and retainers. From the patio a stair leads to the dependencies on the second floor to the east and to the great hall on the west. Between the two areas, on the same stair, is the kitchen with its great fireplace, counters, water supply, and even a hole for garbage disposal. The great hall is a magnificent rib-vaulted chamber. The ribs of the vault at the north end where the high table stood are elaborately carved with floral and geometric motifs. Corbels in the massive walls support the ribs. These corbels are decorated with secular scenes of a banquet in progress including the benediction, the seated guests being served bread, wine, and covered dishes, handwashing with basins and towels, and entertainment by musicians and jugglers. That the palace was fortified and provided with heavy doors, we know from descriptions of civil wars in the *Historia Compostelana.* That Archbishop Gelmírez had private retiring rooms and was in the habit of taking a siesta we also know from the accounts of the uprising of 1136. Of the other fine houses of canons, nobles, or burghers, nothing remains. Undoubtedly the episcopal palace outshone them all and reflects the royal palaces of the time rather than the more humble domestic architecture.

The cathedral school was evidently located in the palace. The list of the cathedral doors given in the *Pilgrims' Guide* includes one called the "grammar school door" in the north aisle opposite the palace. (In the ninth-century plan of a monastery in the library at St. Gall the abbot's residence was on the north side of the church and with it were the school and facilities for wealthy guests.) The dependencies of the cathedral were arranged like a monastery around a cloister. The canons of the cathedral could live in their own homes, if they had them, but communal residential facilities, including dormitory and refectory, were provided around the cloister. Nothing remains of the canonry.

Before public buildings were built in Santiago in the thirteenth century, citizens met in private houses, in squares, or in the porches or cloisters of the churches. The authors of the *Historia Compostelana* describe political meetings in the cloisters of monasteries and even in the canonry. Business was transacted in large domestic halls donated to the guilds by wealthy citizens. López Ferreiro calculated that by the end of the Middle Ages over twenty guilds had built halls in Santiago, and many of them also had guest rooms in the guild halls. (Certainly in the thirteenth century the shoemakers had an inn.)

The vernacular architecture we would so like to learn more about today was of little interest to the medieval traveler, and our twelfth-century guide is not distracted by the wonders and hazards of Compostela. Immediately after listing the gates, he lists, without any description, the churches of the city—the cathedral, two abbeys, and seven parish churches, one of which had a cemetery for pilgrims. The parish churches have been rebuilt although St. Felix and Sta. Suzanna still have their twelfth-century façades. The monastic churches have disappeared, being replaced in the Renaissance and Baroque periods by the splendid establishments which now fill the city.

The typical church was basilican in form with nave and side aisles, often a transept and apse, oriented east-west with the altar at the east. The church usually had side entrances into the transepts or side aisles as well as a western portal. A pair of towers might flank the façade, and a low tower often marked the crossing of nave and transepts or the sanctuary. In most elaborate churches the interior space might be divided into aisles by columns with carved capitals, and the crossing of nave and transept might be covered by an octagonal lantern tower on squinches, which lighted the sanctuary. The high altar in the apse was often supplemented by side altars in lateral chapels, which were usually arranged in an echelon plan. Only the most elaborate and important churches had an ambulatory with radiating chapels.

The Spanish builders had a strong preference for masonry construction. Their fine ashlar masonry churches are excellent examples of the functional architecture of the southern builders found in Spain, southern France, and Italy.

Romanesque architecture was based on Roman building as interpreted by early Christian and Byzantine architects, but was also strongly influenced by local traditions and materials —in Spain by Visigothic, Asturian, Lombard, Mozarabic, and Moorish styles. Masons traveled from place to place across northern Spain working on the largest and finest buildings, while the simpler churches were built by local craftsmen. Thus on both sides of the Pyrenees a style evolved characterized by technical excellence and functional planning. The masons seemed to be following the early twentieth-century precepts such as "truth to materials" and "form follows function"; however, they did not intend to be as "true" to their materials as modern restorations would have them. The taste of the twelfth century, with the exception of the more austere religious orders such as the Cistercian, tended toward opulence. Churches were richly decorated and furnished, the greater to glorify God (as Abbot Suger of St. Denis in France so effectively explained) but also to satisfy the taste of the great patrons.

Sculptors elaborated the doorways and the capitals of columns especially in the cloisters, and painters covered the fine stone walls with decorative and instructive paintings inspired by Byzantine mosaics and Constantinian paintings in the basilicas of Rome. In the apse the awe-inspiring image of Christ in majesty loomed over the worshiper. On the walls the drama of the lives of the saints or the horrors of Hell and the joys of Heaven were represented. Occasionally the Virgin and Child might preside over a heavenly court, but in the twelfth century these figures, too, were hieratic images, imperial figures receiving the homage and the gifts of the Magi. While all the large wall spaces were filled with edifying narratives, the purely architectural members, such as columns or ribs of vaults, were decorated with geometric patterns in pure, bright colors: white, yellow, red, black. The painters might cover a column with wavy lines of varying colors, clearly hoping to create the effect of the colored marbles they had seen or heard about in Roman and Asturian buildings. After all, the Compostelan basilica of Alfonso III had had a veneer of green, black, white, and red marble. In Galicia, where a fine grayish-white marble was available, the granite buildings were decorated with columns and reliefs of that lovely material.

The interior of the buildings were also hung with rich textiles, and the altars had golden frontals, baldachinos, of silver, gold, and enamel, glass and metal lamps, crosses and reliquaries. When rich materials were beyond the means of the church, as splendid an effect as possible was achieved with painted and gilded wood and stucco. Thus the Romanesque builder and his patron did their best to recreate the splendors of an imperial court of heaven in the mountains of Navarre or the valleys of Galicia.

The problem of the Christian architect or builder is twofold: as in other religions he must provide an earthly home for his God, but unlike many, especially early religions, he must also provide facilities to house the entire religious community during worship. The building must be a magnificent shrine to the glory of God and still a practical architectural setting for the sacrificial drama of the Christian liturgy, including suitable areas for preparation of the priests and safekeeping of liturgical vessels. At the same time the building must be large enough to house a large congregation in a large, open area so that they may witness the divine drama and participate in the worship service. Furthermore the cult of relics and veneration of local saints added further complexity because a church might have to commemorate not only one but several saints. In a major cathedral like

Santiago de Compostela, not only St. James, but St. Andrew, St. Peter, and others, each had his altar. As our guide tells us:

"The altars of the basilica are found in this order: first after the French door on the left, the Altar of St. Nicholas; then the Holy Cross; then off the ambulatory the altar of St. Foy the Virgin; then the altar of our Savior in the large central apsidal chapel; following, altar of the Apostle Peter; then the altar of St. Andrew; then of St. Martin the Bishop; then St. John the Baptist. Between the altar of St. James and the altar of the Saviour is the altar of St. Mary Magdalene where the early morning masses for the pilgrims are sung. Above in the gallery of the church are three altars, the principal of which is dedicated to the Archangel Michel and another to the right is dedicated to St. Benedict and another to the left to the Apostle Paul and to St. Nicholas the Bishop; up there the archbishop's chapel is also found." (Book V, Chapter IX)

As if this were not problem enough for the master mason or cleric in charge of the building, churches along the pilgrimage road had to be prepared for crowds of people arriving at irregular intervals. In the Cathedral of Santiago the traffic problem threatened to destroy the dignity of the services when everyone wanted to participate in services and prayers at once.

Simply stated, the church had to be thought of as being in two parts, fulfilling the two functions defined earlier; that is, the sanctuary with its dependencies for the clergy and a hall for the congregation. The apse provided a semi-circular area around the altar and space for the clergy, to which a room at each side might be added for the storage of equipment and the preparation for the ritual. With the growth in numbers of clergy—especially with the development of monastic churches—the area of the sanctuary was enlarged until it might approach the nave in size. More relics of saints required more altars, each within its own setting so that around the sanctuary a cluster of chapels had to be organized. When only three or five altars were needed, they could be lined up in a row, but such an arrangement became cumbersome when more were involved. As the cult of relics developed, the natural desire of the worshiper to get as close as possible to the object of his veneration, even to try to touch it, added an entirely new aspect to the already difficult problem of providing for both a congregation and the clergy.

This problem was solved by building a passageway around the principal altar, off which other altars could be placed in individual, independent chapels. This arrangement of an ambulatory, as the passage was called, with radiating chapels, around the high altar, enabled the pilgrim to visit each chapel in turn in an orderly fashion, and also provided access to the crypt and tomb of the saint from the sides or from behind. The transept also provided additional space near the altar. Aisles increased the size of the nave. In the pilgrimage church, aisles were continued around the transepts and led to chapels on the east side of the transepts and connected with the ambulatory and radiating chapels around the altar. The pilgrims could enter the cathedral and visit each chapel in turn without ever moving out into the center of the nave or transept. To provide even more space, the aisle area was doubled by providing a gallery over aisles and ambulatory; this same gallery acted as a buttress to the high barrel vaults.

The crowds of people to be accommodated are described in a sermon supposedly preached by Pope Calixtus on the Feast of the Translation of St. James:

———————

"The contemplation of the choirs of pilgrims in perpetual vigilance at the foot of the venerable altar of Santiago causes both joy and admiration: the Germans on one side, the French on another, the Italians on another; they are in groups with burning candles in their hands; the entire church is lighted by them as if by the sun on a clear day. . . . Some play citherns, others lyres, others dulcimers, others flutes, recorders, trumpets, harps, viols, British or Welsh wheels; some sing with citherns; others sing accompanied by various instruments; all spend the night in vigils; others weep for their sins; others read the psalms; others give alms to the blind. In the church one hears various languages and voices in barbaric tongues, conversations and songs in German, English, Greek, and the languages of other tribes and diverse people of every region of the world. The word or the language does not exist in which voices do not resound. These vigils are meticulously celebrated; some come, others go, offering a variety of gifts. If one comes in sad, he leaves happy. . . .

"The doors of this basilica are never closed, by day or by night; nor does the darkness of night find a place in there; for the light shines from the candles and tapers as brilliantly as noonday. To Santiago come the poor, the rich, the criminals, the knights, the princes, the governors, the blind, those without arm or hand, the powerful, the nobles, the heroes, the primates, the bishops, the abbots, some barefoot, others penniless, others laden with iron or lead for the work on the basilica of the Apostle; others, weeping for their sins, liberated from the prisons of tyrants, carry the iron chains and manacles as penance on their shoulders; they have been freed by the intercession of the Apostle." (*Codex Calixtinus,* Book I, chapter XVII)

———————

The Romanesque master mason and architect built in stone, which provided both the permanence and dignity the builder wished to achieve. It was relatively fireproof, an important consideration when religious rites emphasize candle-lit altars and processions with torches. Furthermore, a stone church could be a stronghold in time of distress, providing the community with a fortress in both the physical and the spiritual sense. The use of stone conferred on the structure a dignity necessary for the house of God, setting it apart from the houses of the townspeople and making it the equal if not the superior of the castles and palaces of the temporal lords. The social status indicated by building in stone can be noted in occasional references to wealthy or important burghers who owned stone houses. Finally, stone construction was aesthetically satisfying and particularly important in achieving the acoustical effects desirable in the age of the plain song. Music was cultivated in Santiago de Compostela, and the importance of cathedral music is reflected in the sculpture of the cathedral and recorded in the music of the Calixtine Codex.

The technique of stone masonry had never died out in Spain as it did in some places. After the fall of the Roman Empire, Roman building techniques were continued on a small scale by the Visigoths (who were not above borrowing stones from ruined Roman buildings). Even after the Moorish invasions, the Christians in the mountain strongholds of Asturias continued to build vaulted structures. In Catalonia vaulting was further developed in the early eleventh century, and from the Catalan and Lombard regions the technique of stone masonry, using round arches and barrel and groin vaults, spread back through western Europe. By the last quarter of the eleventh century builders worked with a skill which rivaled the Romans.

A small church might consist of a single aisle with heavy walls supporting and buttressing the thrust of the vault and ending in a semicircular or square vaulted or semi-domed sanctuary. The larger church required a more complex system of support. The largest, the Cathedral of Santiago de Compostela, was entirely vaulted; the high nave, transept and choir were covered with a barrel vault raised on massive piers and articulated by ribs. The aisles had groin vaults and supported galleries which were covered by quadrant vaults, which in turn carried the powerful thrust of the nave vault out and down to the outer walls of the building. This system of vault supporting vault required massive stone walls and permitted only relatively small windows; however, it was quite strong, and a building thus constructed was able to withstand centuries of use and abuse by man and the elements.

This style in architecture was not confined to one medieval kingdom. The sheer mobility of the population made possible the exchange of ideas and even the travel of individual workmen and artists. Much ink has been wasted in the debate over the French or Spanish origin of the style, a debate which any medieval mason would consider ludicrous. Whether he was constructing a church in Aragón, a bridge in Navarre, a castle in León, or the Cathedral of Santiago de Compostela or the Church of St. Sernin in Toulouse, the mason built in the massive, dignified, sturdy, functional round-arched, barrel-vaulted stone masonry which was his style, the style of the Christian states, of the Pilgrims, of St. James, of the Crusade, of the twelfth century.

The Cathedral of Santiago de Compostela has not survived as a pure example of the early Romanesque pilgrimage style. The fabric was altered even in the twelfth century by the addition of the magnificent *Pórtico de la Gloria,* and the church was further fortified and then completely encased in Renaissance and Baroque chapels, cloister, and other dependencies. Now only the south portal retains some of its original exterior appearance. The mighty Romanesque fabric of the interior still dominates the Baroque altars. Unfortunately the Romanesque choir, altar, ciborium, and shrine have been removed, and except for fragments of the choir they are lost. The *Pilgrims' Guide* is our best source of information about the appearance of the cathedral in the early twelfth century. Much of the description in the *Guide* is of interest primarily to the student of architectural history and can be found in Kenneth John Conant's excellent early book on the Cathedral of Santiago.

The *Guide* tells us:

"The master masons who began the construction of the basilica of St. James were named don Bernardo, the elder, an admirable master, and Roberto, and they were assisted by about fifty other stone masons who worked assiduously there during the administration of the very faithful don Wicarto, don Segeredo, prior of the canons and the Abbot don Gundesindo, during the reigns of Alfonso [VI] King of Spain, and of Diego the first, a valiant knight and generous man. The church was begun in the era 1116 [1078] . . . and from the year in which the first stone of the foundations was laid until the last stone was placed, forty-four years passed. From the moment when it was begun until today this church has shone with the light of the miracles of St. James; in it, health was given to the sick,

53

sight was restored to the blind, speech to the mute, hearing was given to the deaf, a normal stride was given to the lame, the possessed were delivered, and even more important, the prayers of the faithful were answered, their wishes accomplished, the chains of sin fell away, the heavens opened to those who called, consolation was given the afflicted and all the foreign peoples coming from all parts of the world gathered here in a crowd bringing their presents and their praises to the Lord." (Book V, chapter IX)

In describing the appearance of the cathedral, the *Guide* says:

"There will be nine towers on this church; that is, two over the portal of the fountain; two over the south portal; two over the west portal; two over the stairs; and another larger one surmounting the crossing in the middle of the church. With these and other very beautiful details the basilica of St. James shines in magnificent glory. It is entirely built of strong, living stone, dark brown and hard as marble; on the interior it is painted in different ways, and on the exterior it is perfectly covered with tiles and lead. But of all this of which we have spoken, part is completely finished and part is yet to be completed." (Book V, chapter IX)

The sheer numbers of people to be accommodated at services, at private devotions, and in "tour groups" provided the architect with problems and gave rise to brilliant solutions. The pilgrim also presented a challenge to the sculptors and painters who were called upon to embellish the church. A distinctive style in the figurative arts developed along the pilgrimage road, like the architect's style reflecting the special requirements of the pilgrims. The sculptor or painter did not need to worry about the number of people in the building as did the architect; but he did have to be concerned with the kind of audience his work would have, an audience unusual in the Middle Ages. The feudal lords and princes of the church were truly mobile, and they traveled incessantly. The merchants (whose number was steadily increasing), the traveling entertainers, and the armies moved about the country. On the other hand, the peasant was tied to the land; the craftsman, to castle or town; the monk, to his monastery. Any of these people might become pilgrims, however, and pilgrims in large numbers visited major shrines along relatively specific routes.

The monastic artist had lavished great care on every detail of his work; work meant to be studied closely, perhaps for the lifetime of the viewer. The artist at work on the pilgrimage church, on the other hand, was called upon to create a work of art to be seen only once or twice by any single individual. He had to make an immediate impact; his sculpture or painting had to tell its story at a glance. It must have a message of importance, but one which did not require a subtle interpretation or lengthy contemplation. It must be stunning enough to make the pilgrim feel the trip was worth while. Needless to say, the theme of giving is important; the three Magi often appear; the virtues of poverty and vice of avarice are constantly represented as in the story of Lazarus and the rich man; and Christ and the local saints are equated triumphantly. The style of the sculpture and painting is broad and realistic within the terms of the abstract Romanesque style. Stories are told with great economy of means but with considerable dramatic force, much like the art of the present-day comic strip. The images are impressive and intelligible to the man on the road as well as to the erudite abbot or bishop. No better example can be found than the sculpture of the Cathedral of Santiago; and the description of the twelfth-century visitor, with his interest in the stories, brings this home:

———————

"The south portal of the Apostolic Basilica is composed, as we have said, of two doors with four valves. On the door at the right, on the exterior, in the first register above the door the Betrayal of Christ is carved in a remarkable fashion. There Our Lord is tied to the column by the hands of the Jews; there He is beaten with cords; there Pilate sits on his throne to judge Him. Above, in another register, the Blessed Mary, Mother of Our Lord, is carved with her Son in Bethlehem, and there are also the three kings who come to visit the Child and His mother, offering to Him their three gifts, and the star, and the angel who warns them not to return to Herod. On the jambs of this same door are two Apostles as guardians one to the right, the other to the left. The same is true of the left door, there are two other Apostles on the jambs. And in the first register above the entrance, the Temptation of Our Lord is carved. In front of Christ there are some frightful angels resembling monsters who place Him on the summit of the temple; others present Him with stones inviting Him to change them to bread; others show Him the kingdoms of the world pretending that they will give them to Him if He will adore them—such a thing God does not wish. But other good, pure angels are behind Him and also others above with censors serving Him. . . .

"And one must not forget to mention that next to the Temptation of Christ is a woman holding the head of her lover which was cut off by her own husband who forced her to kiss it twice a day. Oh, what a terrible and admirable punishment of the adulterous woman, which should be told to all!

"In the upper part over the four doors, next to the galleries of the church, is an admirable composition of white marble shining forth magnificently. It is there that one finds Our Lord standing with St. Peter at His left holding the keys in his hand, and St. James at His right between two cypresses with St. John, his brother, next to him, but also to the right and to the left are the other Apostles. Above and below, to the right and the left, the entire wall is magnificently carved with flowers, men, saints, animals, birds, fish, and other works which we cannot describe in detail. And above the arches are four angels with trumpets announcing the Day of Judgment." (Book V, chapter IX)

The cathedral was not quite finished when Aymery visited it, as he mentions in his description of the towers and materials of the building. The west façade must have been under construction because he writes of it in a very laudatory but indefinite fashion, in marked contrast to the detailed descriptions he lavished on the north and south portals.

"The west portal, with its two entrances surpasses the other portals in its beauty, size, and workmanship. It is larger and more beautiful than the others and is even more admirably decorated; many stairs lead up to it outside, and it is adorned by various columns of marble and decorated with various figures and ornaments: images of men, women, animals, birds, saints, angels, flowers, and all kinds of sculpture. Its workmanship is so rich that I cannot describe it in detail. Nevertheless, up above, the Transfiguration of Our Lord is represented as it took place on Mount Tabor, marvellously carved. Our Lord is there in a shining cloud, His face shines like the sun, His clothing shines like snow, and His Father above speaks with Him; and Moses and Elias who appeared at the same time tell Him of His destiny to be fulfilled in Jerusalem. Also St. James is there with Peter and John to whom, before all others, Our Lord revealed His Transfiguration." (Book V, chapter IX)

In Santiago de Compostela, the masterpiece of the pilgrimage style in sculpture was not seen by the writer of the *Pilgrims' Guide*. In 1168, King Ferdinand of León signed a contract with Master Matthew, the master mason of the cathedral, for work on the cathedral at the very handsome salary of two marks of silver a week. Since Master Matthew's name appears in the inscription of 1188 on the lintel of the portal of the west façade, it may be assumed that the unspecified work ordered by the king was the completion of the west façade. The magnificent *Pórtico de la Gloria* still graces the entry to the basilica.

Before the erection of the Baroque façade, the *Pórtico de la Gloria* would have been visible from afar, approached by a long flight of steps. Both inner and outer façades had three large arched openings without door valves. Thus the *Pórtico* was framed by foliage, angels, and interlacing Moorish arches, while it in turn framed the altar and ciborium at the end of the nave. In the *Pórtico de la Gloria* Prophets and Apostles form the columns and jambs leading into the church; and in the center supporting the lintel is a seated figure of St. James welcoming the pilgrims to his basilica. The vault is covered with flowers and supported by angels carrying and leading souls to Paradise, trumpeting the Day of Judgment, and praising the Lord. In the tympanum of the center portal, completed by Matthew's shop, a huge

Christ shows his wounds while angels hold symbols of his passion and souls in Paradise sing his praises.

We have only the description in the *Pilgrims' Guide* for our knowledge of the magnificent sanctuary of the cathedral:

———————

"Up to now we have spoken of the characteristics of the church, now we must treat of the venerable altar of the Apostle. According to tradition, in the venerable basilica reposes the revered body of St. James, over which a magnificent high altar was raised in his honor; he lies in a tomb of marble in a very beautiful vaulted sepulchre of admirable work and just dimensions. Also it is believed that his body is immovable, according to the testimony of St. Teodomiro, bishop of the city, who discovered it in past times and was not able to move it. Ignore the rivals from over the mountains who say they have something of him or his relics. Actually the body of the Apostle is entirely here, divinely illuminated by heavenly rubies, constantly honored with fragrant and divine perfumes, lighted by celestial candles and honored and surrounded by guardian angels. And over his sepulchre is a modest altar which, it is said, was made by his own disciples and which for the love of the Apostle and his disciples, no one has wanted to destroy. And above him is a large admirable altar which measures five palms in height, twelve in length, and seven in width. I have measured it with my own hands.

"The small altar is enclosed under the larger one on three sides, that is, on the right, the left, and behind; but it is not covered in front so that one can clearly see the old altar when the altar frontal of silver is removed. And if someone through devotion to St. James should wish to send a drapery or a cloth to cover the altar of the Apostle, it should be made nine palms wide and twenty-one long; on the other hand, if one should wish for the love of God and the Apostle, to send a frontal to cover the altar in front, one should see that its width is seven palms and its length thirteen.

"The Silver Frontal

"The frontal then, which is in front of the altar, is magnificently worked in gold and silver. In the middle is carved the throne of our Lord surrounded with twenty-four elders arranged in the same order that St. John, brother of St. James, saw them in the Apocalypse, that is to say, twelve to the right and the same to the left, all in a circle, holding in their hands cithers and vases of gold filled with perfumes. In the middle sits Our Lord as on a throne of majesty having in his left hand the Book of Life and giving a blessing with His right. Around the throne as if to sustain it, are the four Evangelists. The twelve Apostles are arranged to the right and left, three on the first row to the right and three above. Similarly on the left there are three in the first row below and three above. Beautiful flowers are placed all around and very beautiful columns separate the Apostles. This frontal of perfect and splendid workmanship is engraved above with this inscription in verse: 'Diego II [Gelmírez] Bishop of Santiago had this frontal made in the fifth year of his Bishopric [1105]. It cost the treasury of Santiago seventy-five marks of silver minus five.' And below this other inscription is found: 'The King was then Alfonso, his son-in-law, Duke Raymond, when the above mentioned prelate finished the work.'

"The Ciborium of the Altar of the Apostle

"The Ciborium which covered this venerable altar is admirably decorated on the interior and on the exterior with paintings, drawings, and various images. Square in plan, it rests on four columns and is made with good proportions of height and width. On the interior, in the first register one finds eight figures of women representing the virtues particularly celebrated by St. Paul. In each corner there are two, and over their heads some angels stand holding with their raised hands a throne which is at the top of the ciborium. In the center of the throne one finds the Lamb of God holding a cross with his foot. There are as many angels as virtues. On the exterior, in the first register, four angels play their trumpets to announce the Resurrection and the Day of Judgment. Two are on the front face and two behind. At the same level there are four precursors, Moses and Abraham on the left face and Isaac and Jacob on the right; each has in his hand a scroll with his individual prophecies.

"In the upper register, the twelve Apostles are seated in a circle. First, the front face, St. James is seated in the center, holding a book in his left hand and giving his blessing with his right. At his right is another Apostle and at his left a second in the same row. In the same way on the right face of the ciborium there are three other Apostles, and three others on the left and also another three on the back. Above, on the roof, four angels are seated as if they were guarding the altar; but on the four corners of the ciborium, at the base of the roof, the four Evangelists are carved with their own symbols. The interior of the ciborium, on the other hand, is painted, while on the exterior it is sculptured and painted. On the summit on the exterior is placed a little monument with a triple arcade in which the Holy Trinity is carved. Under the first arch, which faces west, is the person of the Father; under the second toward the southeast is the Son; and under the third toward the north is the person of the Holy Spirit. Also at the very summit, is a resplendent ball of silver over which is elevated a precious cross.

"The Three Lamps

"In front of the altar of St. James three large silver lamps are suspended in honor of Christ and the Apostle. The one in the center is very large and is admirably worked in the form of a large mortar. It is composed of seven receptacles representing the seven gifts of the Holy Spirit where the seven lamps are placed. The receptacle receives only the oil of balsam, or myrtle, or Indian myrtle, or olive. The receptacle in the center is larger than the others. On the outside of each of those which surround it, two figures of Apostles are carved. May the soul of Alfonso, king of Aragón [d. 1134], who, it is said, gave it to St. James, rest in eternal peace.

"At the altar of St. James mass is celebrated only by a bishop, archbishop, pope, or cardinal of the church. Actually, there are ordinarily seven cardinals in this basilica who celebrate the divine office on that altar. They were created and recognized by many pontifs and also have been confirmed by Pope Calixtus. This dignity, which the basilica of St. James possesses by excellent right out of regard for the Apostle, cannot be taken away." (Book V, chapter IX)

The writer of the *Pilgrims' Guide* summarizes the superior qualities of the cathedral in one of the few evaluations of the effect of architecture written in the Romanesque period:

"In this church there is not a crack, not a fault; it is admirably constructed, large, spacious, light, of harmonious dimensions, well proportioned in length, breadth, and height, and of the most admirable structural soundness because it is constructed in two stories like a royal palace. He who walks around the galleries, although he may have been sad when he climbed up there, becomes consoled and happy as he looks at the perfect beauty of this church." (Book V, chapter IX)

IV.
History and Politics
in Santiago de Compostela

Before daily life in Santiago de Compostela is discussed, a brief history of the city and its hinterland may prove useful. Alfonso VI, during his long reign (1065–1109), almost succeeded in creating a stable central government based on a loose interpretation of the feudal system. Had he been able to rise above personal jealousy and petty intrigue, he could have been the ruler of a powerful, united empire. Alfonso's early reign was one of continuous military triumph, culminating in the conquest of Toledo in 1085; however, his later years were marred by defeats at the hands of the Amoravides. Only *el Cid Campeador,* Rodrigo Díaz de Vilar, one of the great military leaders of the Middle Ages, could contain and even defeat these new Moorish invaders from the Sahara. Alfonso never achieved a permanent reconciliation with this great friend and supporter of his murdered brother, Sancho. Because of Alfonso's continued antagonism, *el Cid* set up his own kingdom in Valencia and eventually allied himself with the growing Catalan power of his son-in-law, Count Raymond Berenguer.

Alfonso VI did, however, maintain a successful policy in relation to France. He married (in succession) Ines of Aquitaine, Constance of Burgundy, and then three more

French women. He was a loyal supporter of the powerful French monastery of Cluny; his confessor and the primate of Spain, the archbishop of Toledo, was a Cluniac. Alfonso and the monks of Cluny were responsible for the introduction of the Roman rite, as well as French culture, into Spain. Cluniac monks established important houses in Spain, especially along the road to Santiago de Compostela, and were powerful advocates of the pilgrimage to the tomb of the Apostle. Alfonso generally maintained a policy of close relations with western Europe, breaking the isolationist course of Mozarabic Spain.

The problem of the succession after Alfonso VI was important in the history of the city of Santiago de Compostela. Alfonso's two daughters, Urraca and Teresa, married two Burgundian counts, Raymond of Burgundy and Henry of Lorraine, both nephews of Queen Constance. The noblemen had come to the peninsula as crusaders and remained there; and Raymond, who married Urraca in 1088, was especially notable for his total commitment to the kingdom. He surrounded himself with local men, and he remained resolutely loyal to Alfonso VI and his adopted country. Alfonso made Raymond and Urraca rulers of Galicia, while he gave Portugal to Henry and Teresa.

The legal situation and the position of Galicia in the early twelfth century was extremely complex and conducive to anarchy. First Raymond and Henry made a pact inspired by the abbot of Cluny: if Raymond, through Urraca, should inherit the kingdom of León-Castile, Henry would receive the valuable land of Toledo as a fief; however, the treasury of Toledo would be divided between them with Raymond taking two-thirds. Unfortunately for the political stability of the realm, Raymond died prematurely in 1106 or 1107.

Another pact was made by the archbishop of Vienne

(Raymond's brother and later Pope Calixtus II) and witnessed by his friend Bishop Gelmírez that Urraca and her son by Raymond, Alfonso Raimundez, were to rule Galicia jointly in subordination to the crown, but if Urraca were to remarry, she would lose her sovereignty and her son Alfonso would be sole lord. The nobles took an oath to uphold this pact in León in 1107.

Then in the next year the heir apparent, Prince Sancho, was killed in the disastrous battle of Uclés. Urraca, next in line of succession, was proclaimed heir apparent and the nobles swore allegiance to her. Her son was to rule Galicia as her vassal. Needless to say the authors of the *Historia Compostelana* do not mention this later oath since they were to claim that Urraca lost her sovereignty when she remarried.

Alfonso VI's death in 1109 and the marriage of Urraca to Alfonso el Batallador, king of Aragón, almost at once brought the problem to a head. Urraca and Alfonso made each other co-rulers, but Alfonso Raimundez was to succeed them if they had no children. Since Alfonso and Urraca were cousins and had not received a dispensation, their marriage could be considered illegal. Furthermore, they were completely incompatible. The story of the next few years is one of crisis, dissention, and political anarchy. The Galician nobles, led by Alfonso Raimundez' tutor, the Count of Traba, proclaimed him king of Galicia in 1109; and he was crowned in the Cathedral of Santiago de Compostela by Gelmírez in 1111. He did not, however, become king of León as Alfonso VII until his mother's death in 1126.

With central government disrupted, the people depended on themselves for protection. Leagues and brotherhoods were formed by nobles, by peasants, and by townsmen for self-protection but also to wage war on each other. Town councils were granted charters giving them the administrative and judicial powers formerly held by a feudal lord. The position of the bishop of Santiago de Compostela in this period was extremely difficult because of his responsibilities as a secular lord as well as a religious leader. For example, the nobles founded a brotherhood in 1109 when Gelmírez as titular head. Later, however, Gelmírez was able to free himself from the nobles and supported the young prince, Alfonso VII. He maintained this allegiance to Alfonso VII through the many changes of fortune and friendship of the early twelfth century.

The history of the city of Santiago de Compostela is that of a constant struggle between the bishop who tried to maintain his absolute authority and the people who wanted self-government. The lower classes had little to lose and were always ready for a fray. The wealthy burghers hoped for greater civil rights. Suppression by the vicars, sheriffs, and militia only added to the pressures; and civil disobedience had a real meaning and purpose in twelfth-century Santiago de Compostela. Even a relatively benevolent dictator was still a dictator. The burghers saw free cities founded directly under the king and envied the councils of these royal towns, for the possibilities of self-government were much stronger under a king who was usually absent than under either a lay or ecclesiastical lord in residence.

One of the great advantages of city life was the freedom it offered as compared with the position of the peasant bound to the land. Naturally the more aggressive and adventurous spirits were attracted to this life. A serf staying in a city for forty days gained his freedom. In Santiago de Compostela the influx of pilgrims also added to the ferment and, literally, to the free population.

Nominally the citizens of Compostela were free men; they had been granted their freedom by Ordoñiz II in 915.

By the mid-eleventh century, however, there were many residents whose actual status was doubtful. A group known as *juniores* or *foreros* were neither free nor unfree. They still owed contributions to their lords and could not change their residence at will; yet they were living and working in Compostela. In 1105 the inhabitants of the city were given a new charter in which all residents of the city at that date were free men under the bishop of Santiago. They were exempt from fines for not answering the call to military service, from payment of inheritance taxes, from taxes on giving daughters in marriage or having marriages annulled. They were exempt from the lord's exclusive right to stamp and seal documents and from giving security worth more than five sueldos; they were exempt from military service unless they could come and go on the same day. They were authorized to pursue criminals and were exempt from answering for crimes committed in the city. They were declared subject only to God, St. James, and the clergy, but as free men. (The charter is referred to in Book I, chapter 23 of the *Historia Compostelana* and is reproduced in López Ferreiro, Vol. II, appendix XIX.)

Each step in the direction of greater freedom and civil rights encouraged the burghers to press for more. And as long as the archbishop saw that it was clearly in his best interests, he granted more and greater privileges. The archbishop began to establish a government under which a twelfth-century city could flourish. As is so often the case, he moved too slowly. The inhabitants of older feudal cities such as Compostela envied the citizens of royal cities. They felt that they would have greater opportunity for self-government and the development of their enterprises under the rule of a monarch whose attention would usually be directed elsewhere than under the constant supervision of a resident bishop. Thus, by 1116, the citizens of Santiago felt that they had lost their formerly enviable position and were instead being deprived of their just rights. Leaders among them were ready to stir up insurrection in hopes of achieving their goals in one bloody stroke rather than establishing their rights and powers gradually over the years.

The twelfth century became a period of civil disorder with bloody confrontations between burghers and archbishops. The first of these uprisings occurred in 1117 when the community openly and violently challenged the authority of Gelmírez and Queen Urraca. A dramatic account, written by partisans of the bishop, is found in Book I, chapters 114, 115, and 116 of the *Historia Compostelana.* These chapters reflect the excitement of the events, and they also illustrate the vivid narrative style of the best twelfth-century historians. Chapter 114 describes the uprising of the people and the burning of the cathedral. Stirred to a frenzy by rumors of reprisals, the citizens of Compostela joined the traitors in an attack on Queen Urraca and Gelmírez in the bishop's palace.

———————————

"The Bishop and the Queen, who were living in the palace, heard the clamor and din in the city and realized the degree to which the traitors, imitators of Iscariot, had incited the citizens against them. . . . The Church of the Apostle was attacked; over the altar flew stones, bolts, lances; the traitors delivered sacrilegious blows. What did those evil hands not dare! The perverse aggressors set fire to the Church of Santiago; from one side to the other it began to burn, for much of it was covered with wooden planks and straw mats [because it was still under construction and the stone vault was not finished]. Oh evil! That a church so venerable and so worthy of an Apostle should be burned, and that such a precious Patron should not be honored. Oh grief! The flames reached the highest part of the Apostolic Church and everywhere presented a horrifying spectacle. . . . the pilgrims from many lands who had come to visit the shrine of the Apostle shed floods of tears!

"Thus it was that the Bishop and the Queen saw that the church was burning and that the conspirators were soon ready to perpetrate every evil, and thus they did not consider themselves safe in the Bishop's palace, and with all their followers they took refuge in the bell tower. The citizens, in their turn, climbed to the upper part of the church and entered the Bishop's palace, ruining, robbing, destroying clothing and vases of gold and silver and everything else that belonged to the Bishop and the Queen. . . . Finally they went up into the Church of the Blessed Apostle, climbed the tower of the Bishop's palace and began an assault on the bell tower where the Bishop with his followers and knights and the Queen with her men had taken refuge. . . . the citizens realized that the small band could resist their multitude, and the success of the fight hung in the balance, and they decided to use fire; and protecting their heads with their shields, they were able to start a fire through a low window in the tower. They heaped on the fire everything that would burn. . . .

"The Queen then turned to the Bishop and said, 'Leave here, Father, leave this fire that I may go with you; because you as patron, Bishop, and lord will be spared.' The Bishop replied, 'That is not good advice, because it is I and my relatives that they consider enemies, and our death is what they really want.' At this those outside shouted, 'Let the Queen leave if she wishes; we will give permission to leave and to live only to her; the others shall perish by iron and fire.' Hearing this, and as the fire increased in the tower, the Queen, encouraged by the Bishop and having obtained assurance from those outside, abandoned the tower. But then when the horde saw that she left, they attacked her; they grabbed her and threw her to the ground in a mud hole beating her like wolves; they ripped her clothes to shreds until she lay on the ground on her breast for a long time shamefully naked and in sight of everyone. Many wanted to stone her, and among them an old woman wounded her gravely on the cheek with a stone.

"Meanwhile the Bishop remained praying in the tower, and the fire continued climbing higher. The Abbot of San Martin went to him carrying a crucifix; and having made his confession, he left the tower as though for his martyrdom; and removing his clerical dress and taking from I don't know whom an old worn-out cape, he put the crucifix in front of his face—Oh, admirable thing!—and crossed through the troop that fought, through the ranks of his bloodiest enemies, in the midst of the arms of the most perverse traitors (more than three thousand in number), without being known by more than one. He arrived at the spot where the Queen lay in the mud trampled on by the attackers; and seeing her so hideously naked and exhausted with pain, he passed by at a distance, and through the Church of the glorious Santiago he arrived at the Church of Santa María accompanied by a canon named Miguel González . . . .

". . . Finally the Queen, with her hair dishevelled and her naked body covered with mud, escaped and arrived at the same church where the Bishop was hidden. . . .

"A messenger was secretly sent to the Queen in the Church of Santa María by the Bishop with news of how he had escaped from the fire and was hidden in the same church. Learning this, although weeping for her own shame and pain, she was happy to find the Bishop was safe; but fearing that their persecutors would learn of it, she hid her joy.

"After that, some citizens presented themselves to the Queen congratulating her on her liberation and guaranteeing her safety. To defend her, they filled the church with arms. The Queen, on the one hand fearful of these people and on the other suspicious that they might have learned something of the presence of the Bishop, spoke to them in this manner. 'Go, most perverse ones; go, evildoers to the tower where your Bishop is dying by iron and fire. Snatch him from the danger. Do not be a scandal of evil and infamy for posterity. Go, I repeat, rebels and unbelievers, and avoid committing such a horrible crime.' This she said to make them leave and so that they would not notice the presence of the Bishop. At these words, the people gathered there left and went to the tower; they fought off those who, weapons in hand, were still attacking the tower and adding fuel to the flames. Asking water from all, they threw it into the tower and put out the fire as soon as they could . . . as for the tower, the beams and the planks were all burned; and the bronze bells which weighed fifteen hundred pounds had burned and fallen.

"After the Queen ordered the troops out of the Church of Santa María she left, too, fleeing to the Church of St. Martin for greater safety. The Bishop also left the church without being noticed because of the large number of people. He was accompanied by the above-mentioned Miguel and by two Frenchmen and climbed with his companions over walls and roofs and got in through a window into the house of one Maurino. In a corner of this house the Bishop and Miguel hid themselves under pieces of cloth and other objects. They were thus hidden when four armed men arrived, searching for them, and asked, 'Who is hidden here? What's going on here? Have you seen the Bishop?' . . . But when the men arrived, the two Frenchmen got up and said they had just come from the fray and were tired and resting. At this the lady of the house arrived, knowing that the Bishop was hidden there; and screaming and rebuking the men as robbers and trespassers in her house, she forced them to leave; and finally, so that they would go quickly and the Bishop would not be found, the Frenchmen left with them. . . .

"After the men left, Gonzalo, the son-in-law of the lady of the house, came in saying, 'Father and Lord, fly from here at once and hide! See the infamous troop of rebels, dyed with the blood of the dead but still thirsting for yours, searching for you everywhere; I have seen them with swords and clubs running this way.' . . . the Bishop rose, and Gonzalo made a small hole in the wall between the houses through which they passed, and beyond this another, and then a third, until they arrived inside the house of Froilan Rosende situated in the middle of the city. The owner's wife began to cry out that robbers were destroying and attacking her house. Miguel quieted her, saying that a good friend of her husband . . . had come to take refuge in her house.

"It was not long before the arrival of the owner Froilan Rosende, who, on learning that the Bishop was there, ran to him, saying through his tears, 'Thanks be to God, dearest Father, that you have been freed from such danger, and that you have been brought safely here.' . . . (Rosende hid the Bishop and Miguel in a very dark, underground storeroom.)

"Meanwhile the Frenchmen prepared four very fast horses for the Bishop . . . while these preparations were made, the Abbot of San Pelayo with one of his monks named Pelayo Díaz, and the Prior of the canons, a nephew of the Bishop, arrived on an embassy seeking reconciliation for the traitors. (The Bishop saw through the trick and exposed the perfidy of the citizens.) . . .

"The Abbot returned with the aforementioned monk to the Bishop and told him of the deceit and the lies of the traitors and how well he had foreseen their machinations. Then, as evening was approaching, the Abbot and the monk secretly took the Bishop and Miguel to their church, that is the Church of San Pelayo, where they found accommodations for them in the treasury without letting the monks know, except for the Treasurer. . . . "

Chapter 115 described the activities of the rebels on the following day, Sunday. The rebels gathered in the canons' hall to decide on a course of action. Inspired by the speeches of traitorous former companions of Gelmírez, they decided to make peace with the queen and to declare their independence of the bishop, to divide up the territory of Santiago among themselves, and to establish a city government under a brotherhood. A delegation was sent to the queen with this proposal; and she, in order to escape, pretended to side with the citizens against the bishop. As soon as she had joined her son, who was waiting with his troops outside the city, she sent back word that "such a crime as they [the citizens] had committed could not be left unpunished." The terrified citizens prepared for war, "taking refuge in the church and carrying there all of their most precious possessions."

The daring escape of Gelmírez is described in chapter 116:

"On the same day, Sunday, at sunset the Bishop was in the treasury of San Pelayo thinking about how he was going to be able to escape . . . when a multitude of armed mutineers came running into the cloister of San Pelayo searching for him. Not finding him there, they entered the

74

church, completing the sacrilege. They looked for him in every corner of the church, behind the altars and even under the altar cloths, wishing to take his life if they should find him. . . . the Bishop turned to his companion, 'Let us fly,' he said. 'Miguel, we will leave here at once. You put on this mantle. I will cover myself with this wretched cloak. We shall go quickly with those who are rushing about; and among those who enter and leave, we shall leave ourselves. Only God, if he wishes, can save us.'

"Then the Bishop left with Miguel, between life and death, and passing through the multitude searching for him, he entered the cloister of the same monastery; from there he passed to another cloister, and finding himself walled in, he jumped over a wall near the Church of Santiago near the part next to the altar of San Pedro, and in this manner by crossing over the roof tiles, he arrived, accompanied by Miguel, at the dormitory of our canons, where he was able to rest a little. Then, opening the door of the dormitory, he went to the yard of the palace in front of the refectory. A splendid moon perfectly illuminated all those who ran to the Church of the Apostle carrying their belongings; for then the entire city was terrified for fear of an assault by the army of the queen; and inspired by the knowledge of the crime they had committed, night and day they ran to the church [for sanctuary]. Thus, the Bishop, passing as one of them, arrived at the house of Pedro Gundesindez, Cardinal and Canon of the Church of Santiago, who in spite of many terrible dangers had not moved a jot from the service of his Bishop or from the path of justice.

"Miguel called at the door; the Bishop hid behind him because of the brightness of the moonlight; and the door opened, and the Bishop went into the rooms of the Cardinal, where he remained hidden until some canons left, men whom the Cardinal had invited to supper and who were not in the confidence of the Bishop. But as soon as they left, the Bishop, the Cardinal, and Miguel passed through the house of the Cardinal to another part of the street. Then the Cardinal said to the Bishop, 'Father, it would be better if you were armed, and thus could pass among the sentinels who walk along between here and the trenches as if you were one of them.' 'God does not permit,' responded the Bishop, 'that I should deck myself with arms other than those of Christ, which I have with me. Yesterday I was protected by the arms of Christ; I was freed from the fire and saved from other no less formidable dangers; now guarded by them I will pass with the help and protection of God through the center of my adversaries. Nevertheless, give me two armed men, in whose company I will pass among the sentinels as one of them. Let us go! There is nothing to detain us; because around here the enemies who pursue are waiting and thirst for our blood.'

"Without delay the Cardinal put the advice into execution and gave the Bishop an escort of two armed men. . . . they were seen by two sentinels who were standing at each side and who shouted to them, 'Who is it? Where do you go? What are you looking for?' To these questions one of the men who accompanied the Bishop and who was instructed by him replied, 'We go to the outskirts to explore and reconnoiter and make sure the enemy doesn't attack the city unexpectedly. Now is the time you should be awake and watchful. It is time to move from place to place. You, what are you doing standing still there? How do you get to rest? Get up! Walk and watch with more care!' While saying this they were walking by and jumping the trench. . . .

"Finally the Bishop arrived at Fuente del Roble on the road to Padrón, exhausted from hiking and accompanied by

Miguel and several others, of whom he sent two to a mayor-domo of his who lived near to bring him horses. When these were brought, the Bishop mounted with his companions; and now escorted by a goodly troop of horsemen, he arrived at Iria where he was received by his friends as if he came flying from captivity or had been raised from the dead. . . .

"The Bishop after sending news of his liberty to the Queen from Iria, proclaimed excommunication against all the inhabitants of Compostela and forbade them to enter the Holy Church, an act which terrified the citizens to the marrow of their bones and disheartened them entirely. Immediately he called up the army, all those on foot as well as the cavalry, in the entire province of Santiago; and according to the appeals of the Queen, he came through a blockade around Compostela. The Queen likewise sent messengers everywhere ordering all the nobility, as her knights and servants, to assist at the siege and destruction of Compostela."

The lords supporting the bishop assembled with their troops, and at daybreak the citizens of Compostela found themselves not only "wounded with the sword of anathema" but also surrounded by a host of besiegers with very tangible iron swords. The people set about fortifying the city.

"The traitors went from place to place; fortifying the city with trenches, fences, mountains of stone, bulwarks of wood; rousing and exhorting the people, but in vain. Because then the greater part of the citizens who were not infected with the infamous conspiracy, seeing the city blockaded on all sides, the trees cut, grain harvested, that heads, hands, and feet were chopped off, and the cadavers not buried, also seeing the army of the Queen grow larger and that of the city, smaller ever day, they changed their minds. It could be observed that each night a large number of people deserted, fearful that the city would be entirely destroyed and that its inhabitants would receive what they deserved. Then the traitors began to be hated; no one paid attention to their decisions. . . . Actually, who would not throw himself eagerly on those traitors? . . . Who would not burn those incendiary violators of the Church of the Apostle? All Galicia looked on the authors of such a crime as enemies; all Galicia asked for their blood." (*Historia Compostelana,* Book I, chapters 114, 115, 116)

Thus the revolt was suppressed, but Bishop Gelmírez realized that reforms were necessary. In 1125 he called another council in which the central issue was justice without bribery. Even with the best of intentions on the part of the lord, his sheriffs were usually oppressive; and common people found justice difficult to obtain. Then in 1129 he held yet another council at Palencia, whose decrees, recorded in the *Historia Compostelana* (Book III, chapter 7), give an excellent idea of the range of problems, the abuses, and the corrections and solutions deemed necessary in the period. In the first place, everyone was to obey the king happily and loyally and to give him honest advice. Anyone who did not should be excommunicated.

For church-related problems, bishops were to enforce peaceful agreement, churches were freed from lay authority except with the permission of the bishop and all churches, lands, and serfs were to be restored to their respective sees or monasteries. Churches were not to be given as security; lay investiture was forbidden; and tithes restored to the bishop. Wandering monks were to be given hospitality in the other monasteries and could not be detained by bishops except with the permission of their abbots. Clergy should not be required to bear arms. Excommunicants were not to be received anywhere.

In the realm of private morals, concubinage in the clergy was forbidden, as were adultery and incest among laymen. A group of decrees applied specifically to laymen. Traitors, robbers, rapists, perjurers, and excommunicants were not to be sheltered. Lords should not take the property of their vassals without just cause; counterfeiters were to be excommunicated and blinded; no tolls should be exacted other than those in existence in the time of Alfonso VI, and then they should be for the same amount. Oxen were to be protected from thieves. Finally, "If anyone, intending robbery, attacks the clerics, monks, travelers, merchants, pilgrims visiting sacred places, or women, he shall be imprisoned in a monastery or exiled."

In surveying the history of twelfth-century Santiago de Compostela, the greatest archbishops were undoubtedly Diego Gelmírez who ruled from 1100 to 1139 or 1140 and Pedro Suárez, from 1175 to 1206.

Diego Gelmírez was certainly one of the most remarkable men of the twelfth century. Of course we see him through the eyes of the authors of the *Historia Compostelana* to whom he was the patron and hero. As a churchman, Gelmírez was concerned with both the spiritual and the material body of his church; as a secular lord, he was deeply involved in the power struggles of the emerging kingdom of Castile-León. Always, and as an extension of himself perhaps, the aggrandizement of the cathedral and the city of Santiago de Compostela were primary concerns.

Diego Gelmírez came from a large family and was the son of a member of the minor nobility, the warden of the important Galician fortress, the castle of Torres de Oeste. As a young man, Diego's remarkable ability was noticed by Count Raymond, who in 1092 made him his secretary and notary. So great was Diego's administrative ability and so much confidence did the rulers have in him that twice during the troubled reign of Bishop Diego Pelaez he was made administrator of the see of Compostela. At last, in 1100 while on a trip to Rome, Gelmírez was elected bishop in his own right. He returned to the see at once, and so chaotic were the times that he received special permission to be consecrated in Santiago de Compostela in 1101 rather than to return to Rome for the consecration.

Bishop Gelmírez embarked at once on a campaign to revitalize the church of Santiago de Compostela. He enlarged the cathedral chapter and imposed a strict discipline on the canons. He regularized the church income and provided for the division of the offerings of the cathedral. He encouraged education and foreign travel for study. He strove constantly to establish Santiago as the head of the Spanish church and the leader of Christendom, a role he felt was commensurate with the importance of St. James as the brother of Christ. By 1120 he was able to convince the pope to make Santiago de Compostela an archdiocese, with Salamanca, Braga, and Avila dependent on it. Thereafter he tried to become papal legate and primate of Spain; however, these efforts were consistently frustrated by his rival, the archbishop of Toledo, who already held these positions.

Gelmírez, to achieve his ends, had to come to terms with men from every level of society. His relations with the papacy varied from the very closest, during the reign of Calixtus II (the brother of his former lord, Count Raymond) to genuine mistrust under Innocent II at the end of his reign. His policy was always conciliatory, determined as he was to extract from the incumbent pope the maximum privileges for his see. He was handicapped in his relations by the machinations of his enemies in the papal court, especially by the archbishop of Toledo and his agents, and by his geographical location so far from Rome. To maintain contacts, he and his emissaries had to travel through the hostile territory of the king of Aragón. The stories of their disguises and escapes from the agents of Alfonso of Aragón provide some of the liveliest passages in the *Historia Compostelana.* In spite of all difficulties, Gelmírez attended the church councils and kept pleading the case of his see in the court, freely using huge gifts of gold and silver ("benedictions" as he called them) to smooth his way, to convince the pope and papal court of his good will and loyalty and to gain a position of spiritual supremacy. The almost incredible wealth which Gelmírez was able to accumulate in the see, such a short time after it had been despoiled to the point of bankruptcy by his predecessors, is a testimony to the strength of his administration.

Gelmírez treated the kings Alfonso VI and Alfonso VII in the same way as he did his spiritual lord, the pope; and he was confronted with the same problems and enemies. The king was constantly in financial difficulty and continuously under the influence of the archbishop of Toledo and of courtiers opposed to the Galician party. Gelmírez' policy here, too, was one of negotiation and liberality. Peace had to be kept to insure the steady stream of pilgrims to the city. He gave the king a regular subsidy and made large, extra grants; at the same time he protected the cathedral treasury from the kind of looting which had been going on before he came to power. Even so, the demands of the kings (especially Alfonso VII, whose military projects were unsuccessful) were insatiable; and by the end of his reign Gelmírez was hard pressed to keep up the steady financial support which was necessary to buy favors and security for his people.

Gelmírez' efforts in increasing the material structure of his church met with great success. To him and to his treasurer, Bernardo, the cathedral and city owed their appearance in the twelfth century; for the archbishop shared the enthusiasm for building typical of so many churchmen of the period. He not only pushed forward the construction of the cathedral but also rebuilt churches throughout the city and lands of Compostela. Thus fine granite masonry structures rose to replace the Mozarabic or Asturian buildings of the tenth and eleventh centuries. Like Abbot Suger in France, he employed the best artisans available and was as enthusiastic about the decoration and furnishings of his church and palace as he was about the architecture.

As a secular lord, the archbishop of Santiago was one of the most important nobles in the kingdom and had all the feudal rights and duties that lie with such a position. As we have seen, he was responsible for the executive, legislative, and judicial branches of government; and he permitted a considerable degree of freedom to his subjects. In spite of faults common to his time, he must be judged one of the better lords. His support of the townspeople against the nobility, his encouragement of the commercial and economic development of the city and its hinterland, and the sponsoring of the pilgrimage as a vital force in the life of the people of Galicia may all be considered self-interest. Still, in an era when nobles often sought only to despoil their subjects, such actions were definitely enlightened.

In his efforts to provide protection for Compostela, Gelmírez not only controlled the unruly nobles with his own paid militia, but also may be credited with the founding of the Spanish navy. He had ships built at his own expense to clear the coasts of Galicia of pirates and to wage war and capture booty from the Moors. He made an effort to protect overland travelers along the pilgrimage road, although the Knights of Santiago were not founded until the reign of Pedro Suárez.

Gelmírez' role in the economic rise of Compostela was of crucial importance, for he was determined to develop an economy based on money. With much political maneuvering and shrewd opportunism, he was able to establish his own mint in Santiago. Although the right to coin money had been originally given expressly for work on the cathedral, it was turned to the advantage of the entire population. The existence of an episcopal mint, as well as the influx of pilgrims with money, made Santiago one of the richest cities of the realm and a financial center of major importance.

In 1128 the fortunes of the cathedral and city were much enhanced when lay investiture was abolished and the chapter was granted the privilege of free election of archbishops. Thus the Cathedral of Santiago de Compostela was spared the danger of a royal administrator being imposed if the see was vacant for any period. This was one of the gravest dangers Compostela faced, for these officials in the past had used their office as a way to get their hands on the treasury and to squander the wealth of the cathedral and city.

It is important not to forget the continuing Crusade of the twelfth century and the military role forced upon the archbishop of Santiago in the periods of prestige for the city under Gelmírez and Pedro Suárez. Attention is naturally focused on Toledo, the first great goal of the Crusaders because of its great psychological importance as ancient Visigothic capital as well as its later importance as Primatial See and capital of New Castile; or on Zaragoza, the northern

Moorish capital in the Romanesque period, so bitterly fought for by Aragón and Navarre; or later on the final capture of Córdoba and Seville by St. Ferdinand in the thirteenth century, after the brief occupation of Córdoba by Alfonso in the twelfth century. The role of Santiago de Compostela as a center of pilgrimage is so important that its role in the Crusade is often overlooked.

The importance of the Spanish Crusade is emphasized by the letter of Calixtus II to the churches of western Europe, in 1123, included in the Codex Calixtinus. As an impassioned cry to crusade, it deserves to be included here.

"Calixtus, Bishop, servant of the servants of God, to the bishops, his beloved brothers in Christ, and to the other people of the holy church and to all Christians, present as well as future, universal greetings and Apostolic blessing. You have frequently heard, oh, dearly beloved, of how much evils, calamities, and suffering the Moors have inflicted on our Christian brothers in Spain. No one can count how many churches, castles, and lands they have devastated, and how many Christians—monks, clerics, or laymen—they have killed or sold as slaves in distant and barbarous lands, or probably held in chains and tortured and tormented. It is not possible to tell you in words how many bodies of holy martyrs—that is to say, of bishops, abbots, priests, and other Christians—lie buried near the city of Huesca and in other border territories between Christians and Moors where there have been wars. Thousands are buried!

"For this reason we beg, my sons, that you understand in your charity how important it is to go to Spain to fight the Moors and how many thanks will be given to those who voluntarily go there. Of course, it is known that Charlemagne, king of the Franks, the most famous of all kings, began the Crusade in Spain, fighting the infidels with great effort, and that with his companion the blessed Turpin, archbishop of Reims, according to the story told in his saga, strengthened by the authority of God, in a council of all the bishops of France and Lorraine gathered in Reims, a city of the Franks, conceded a plenary indulgence to all of those who went then or would go later to fight the infidel in Spain, to enhance Christianity, to free Christian captives, and to suffer martyrdom there for the love of God. All of the popes from then until our days have confirmed this, as witness the illustrious holy Pope Urban at the council of Clermont in France attended by one hundred bishops, who assured the indulgence when he preached the crusade to Jerusalem, according to the book of the history of Jerusalem. This same indulgence we ratify and confirm: that all those who go, as we said above, with the sign of the cross of the Lord on their shoulders to fight the infidels in Spain or the Holy Land, will be absolved of all the sins of which they have repented and confessed to their priests; and they shall be blessed by God, the Holy Apostles, St. Peter, St. Paul, and St. James and all the saints and by our apostolic blessing; and they will merit coronation in the celestial kingdom beside the holy martyrs who from the beginning of Christianity until the end of time received or are to receive the palm of martyrdom. Truly no one needed to go there in the past as much as today.

"Therefore it is recommended and universally ordered that all the bishops and prelates in their synods and councils and in the solemnities of the churches shall not fail to announce these apostolic orders first of all; and also they shall exhort the priests in the churches to communicate this to their congregations. And if they do this willingly, they will be rewarded in heaven just as much as those who go on the

Crusade. And anyone who carries a written copy of this letter from one place to another or from one church to another and preaches it to all publicly will be rewarded with eternal glory. Thus those who announce this from here and those who actually go there will have continuous peace, honor, and happiness, victory to the combatants, strength, long life, health, and glory. This is bestowed by Our Lord Jesus Christ, whose reign and empire lasts without end from century to century. Amen. You shall succeed! You shall succeed! You shall succeed!" (The Epistle of Pope Calixtus on the Crusade in Spain, dated March 25, 1123, *Codex Calixtinus,* Book IV, chapter 26.)

In the twelfth century the Spanish Crusade took on a new course. The original Moorish empire had broken up into many smaller kingdoms or Taifas much as the Christian states were divided under feudalism. After the early victories of the Christians, the Islamic leaders of Spain called for help from their fellow religionists in Africa. In 1086 the Almoravides, fanatical nomads from the Sahara, crossed into Spain and led an attack on the Christians which re-established Moorish power across the peninsula. The Moorish cause was helped by dissention among the Christians, the rivalry of Castile, León, Navarre, Aragón, and Catalonia. Although Alfonso VII proclaimed himself emperor of all Spain in 1135, he actually controlled only León, including Galicia, and Asturias and Castile. Raymond Berenguer IV had acquired Aragón in 1140 through his marriage to the daughter of Ramiro of Aragón, but he was Alfonso VII's vassal in name only. In 1139, Portugal was confirmed as an independent kingdom under the heirs of Henry and Teresa. As a final act before he died in 1157, Alfonso VII followed the disastrous precedent of his forebears and divided his kingdom between his sons; Sancho was given Castile and Ferdinand II, León. To further weaken the Christian position another wave of even more fanatical and puritanical Islamic invaders swept in from Africa, the Almohades. They were able to re-establish Moorish power and posed a constant threat to the Christian kingdoms. Thus at mid-century the Iberian peninsula was divided into four centers of power: the Almohade kingdoms, León and Castile, Portugal, and Catalonia-Aragón.

The situation in Compostela was no better than in the peninsula as a whole. After the death of Gelmírez in 1139 or 1140 the city suffered through twenty-eight years of chaos in which six different men held the see for short periods, generally in conflict with the king and nobles. Not until 1168 when Pedro Gudesteiz, bishop of Mondoñedo, former chancellor of Ferdinand II and administrator of the see beginning in 1162, was elected archbishop, was a further peaceful development of the city possible. Although Pedro II lived only five years after his election, his friendship with the king turned the tide of chaos and decay. Santiago de Compostela again received royal support and patronage, and the arts and commerce which had languished for a generation again flourished.

Ferdinand II died in 1188 and was buried in the cathedral. He was followed on the throne by Alfonso IX of León, who ruled from 1188 to 1230. In Castile, Alfonso VIII ruled from 1158 to 1214. Not until Ferdinand III (St. Ferdinand, conqueror of Córdoba and Seville) inherited both León and Castile in the thirteenth century were the kingdoms united again.

Santiago de Compostela experienced a great revival of cultural, commercial, and political life in the last third of the twelfth century. The revival begun by Archbishop Pedro Gudesteiz was continued under the long reign of Archbishop

Pedro Suárez de Deza. Pedro Suárez was a native of Galicia; he had been a canon of the Cathedral of Santiago de Compostela and a student in Paris, a deacon of the cathedral chapter and the bishop of Salamanca. He was elected archbishop in 1173 and ruled for thirty-three years (d. 1206). During his reign the cathedral was finished, although it was not finally consecrated until 1211 during the reign of his successor, Pedro Muñiz.

Pedro Suárez not only completed the material fabric of the cathedral but added enormously to the spiritual and intellectual prestige of the city. He reformed and reorganized the chapter, emphasizing especially education at home and abroad for both clergy and laity. The climax of his reign was the establishment of the Jubilee, a Holy Year still celebrated whenever the feast of St. James falls on Sunday. During that year pilgrims received plenary indulgences and absolution of sins even in cases normally reserved for the papacy. The first Jubilee was celebrated in 1182, and even King Ferdinand II made the pilgrimage.

Pedro Suárez worked hard to restore the material wealth and power of Santiago de Compostela. He insisted on the collection of the *Votos de Santiago,* an ancient nation-wide tax for the cathedral, a thank-offering for the victory of Clavejo. He clarified his jurisdiction over territories and re-established the authority of the archbishop. He had heavy military duties, for after the siege of Cáceres, the Almohades raised a huge army of 78,000 men and a fleet to attack Ferdinand. As a feudal lord of Compostela, Pedro led an army of 20,000 against these invaders at the Battle of Santarén in which Ferdinand was victorious. This was Ferdinand's last triumph, however. The king seems to have fallen into the hands of self-seeking courtiers for the remainder of his reign. Pedro Suárez faithfully served Ferdinand in spite of his fickleness, buried him in the cathedral, and then supported Alfonso IX when he succeeded in 1188. He devoted the last years of his reign under Alfonso IX to the improvement of the economic and political position of the city and territory of Compostela. That the pilgrimage continued with tremendous vigor is indicated by his agreement with the vendors of the scallop shells in which one hundred official vendors were established. The number of shells or badges which must have been sold to require so many official shops is an excellent indication of the great numbers of pilgrims who helped to support the standard of living and a cultural life in Santiago de Compostela at an unprecedented level.

V.
Social Organization, Economic Activity, and Daily Life in the Twelfth Century

Galicia, like the rest of Europe, began the twelfth century as a rural society organized into a tightly structured hierarchy in which wealth and power lay in the hands of great landholders who dominated social, economic, and political life and provided essential military service. By the end of the century, however, the burghers began to challenge and even replace the landholders as a real source of power for the king, just as money replaced barter as the basis of the economy. The people of Santiago de Compostela felt all the strains, the tensions, and the disruption of daily life inevitably produced in a society in transition. While the outward form of the eleventh-century social structure remained, the actual role and importance of each group changed. This gradual change in the power structure probably went unnoticed by the people—certainly the great count of Traba could not foresee that the future lay with people like Froilan Rosende, Miguel Martínez, and Arias Guntádiz, the bread inspectors of Santiago de Compostela.

The Iberian peninsula was divided into distinct and rival political entities: León, of which Galicia was a part, and Castile, which was sometimes united with León; Aragón and Navarre, which were divided into two kingdoms at the death of Alfonso el Batallador in 1134; the county of Catalonia; the county and then kingdom of Portugal; and the Moorish Taifas. León, or León-Castile, was a monarchy, even though after the conquest of Toledo, Alfonso VI called himself emperor. In theory the land belonged to the king under the feudal system; and the nobles received their authority and possessions from the king, who gave them grants of land in return for military and other services. The king's vassals had vassals themselves, who might have vassals in turn; and each vassal was responsible to his immediate superior. Feudalism as it developed in Spain existed more in fact than in law, for the entire nobility recognized the authority of the king, could appeal to him, and were ultimately responsible to him.

The great lords in Spain were the counts, also called "rich men," or palatines. When the title "duke" occurs, it usually refers to a foreign lord such as Raymond of Burgundy or has the military connotation of "general" or "leader of the army." In Spain the counts had legislative, executive, and judicial authority over a territory in return for judicial and legislative assistance at the king's councils twice a year and military service for as much as three months a year. Counts had to maintain an army or at least be prepared to provide a number of troops, which they in turn recruited from their own vassals or paid from taxes. The king retained the right of high justice, the exclusive right to coin money, and control over much legislation, some taxes, and the naming of many officials. Even though the civil government was organized under the hereditary counts, the king had vicars responsible directly to him in independent castles or cities in the counts' territories.

The lesser nobility, the *hidalgos,* were vassals of the upper nobility either living on their own holdings or on money from the count when they were part of his household. The lower class of nobles held executive and judicial—but not legislative—powers; and they were assisted by sheriffs with executive powers only. By the twelfth century these sheriffs were thought of as little better than thieves by the populace. It was their duty to collect taxes, fees, and fines, a duty which they often carried out with excessive, if not illegal, zeal.

Most nobles were a lawless, violent group who oppressed the people in every way. Men of good character such as the count of Traba were rare exceptions to the almost universal rule of greed, faithlessness, and abuse of the weak. The king tried to control the nobles by exacting oaths of peace and loyalty, but these oaths were easily broken. For example, García Pérez kept his word to observe the rights of travelers only three days, and then the temptation presented by a group of merchants from England and Lorraine on the road between Patrón and Compostela proved too much for him. He attacked them and took all their goods and personal possessions.

In Santiago de Compostela complaints were heard and justice done according to the best principles of the day. In the case of García Pérez, he and his men were at once hunted down by the archbishop's army and the citizens' militia. In the ensuing fight some of the robbers were wounded and others taken prisoner, and all the goods were recaptured and restored to the foreign merchants. The best-known account of the judicial procedure of the period is the trial of the counts of Carrión at the court of Alfonso VI in the last book of the *Cantar del Mio Cid.* Here, after the Cid's property was restored, his personal honor was also considered; and in the judicial duel three weeks later the Cid and his family were vindicated and avenged.

The *caballeros,* or knights, were nobles dedicated, with

considerable ritual, to armed service on horseback. In this military age knighthood was the most important and prestigious profession, but in Spain it was clearly a profession and not a class of society. Many regular soldiers were not knights, but all knights were soldiers; knighthood had not become an honorary or decorative title. Theoretically any freeman who could provide himself with horse and armor and who had an annual income of three hundred marks of silver could become a knight. In short, the knights were a privileged group but not a branch of the nobility.

The burghers and many peasants were freemen although they were not noble. The importance of the burghers of Compostela soon became very great. At first a handful of families built their dwellings near the church and monasteries for protection and worked as artisans and traders. How were such people to survive in a system developed for an agrarian society torn by petty raids and wars? As the villages became towns and towns became cities, like Santiago de Compostela, the citizens refused to fit into the simple pattern. The problem was first solved by making the city a unit in the feudal administrative system with the city council holding the executive and even judicial functions of a lord. The lords could not know that these insignificant men, crowded into their town walls and more interested in their silversmithing or shoemaking than in the noble arts of war and the hunt, would slowly and diligently turn them, the great nobles, into a decorative adjunct of an urban industrial society.

A large number of people did not enjoy a free status. One group was neither free nor slave; they had been given partial freedom by their lords but remained attached to the land and to specific service on it. Another group was voluntary serfs—economic or political necessity caused many people to put themselves voluntarily under the protection of a lord or a monastery. The lowest class was composed of slaves who had no control over their destinies or activities. They were the property of their masters; and they could be owned by a lord, a monastery, a rich peasant, or a burgher. They had only one right, that of life; but unlike slaves in many times and places, they could not be killed or mutilated. A person could be born into the slave class or could become a slave as punishment, especially for debt, or through war, as booty. Many slaves were Moors or Jews. Slaves were often among the most creative and productive members of the community, especially those who worked as artisans. They were often given their freedom in return for exceptional services.

An effective government could be provided by city councils. In spite of the fact that they were appointed by the lord, the city councils had a very real power through the ordinances or codes under which they functioned. The council was a relatively independent executive and judicial body. In a free city the council became a feudal lord with jurisdiction over a territory, the right and duty of organizing a militia, and the responsibility for public works such as the building of city walls. To be a "free" city was the goal of the city council of Santiago. By 1136 the burghers were feeling their strength again after the rout of 1117 and again challenged Gelmírez. This time Gelmírez, now an archbishop but older and ailing, was forced to come to terms with them. He acknowledged their claims and accepted their new charter which re-emphasized their right to judicial and legislative powers.

The rights and privileges of the citizens of Santiago de Compostela may seem limited to us today, and some of their problems (for example, wolf hunts) are hard to identify with. Yet if we think of them in a twelfth-century context, we must realize that here were men ready to resort to any means—negotiation, bribery, or open warfare—to establish the right of self-government and personal freedom as they saw it.

Outside the city the free peasants living on the land could have several different relationships to the noble who held the estate. Some peasants had a small private holding although they still paid heavy taxes to the lord. Most were tenants on the lord's land, and still others worked for a salary or maintenance. Each holding was divided between the lord's share and the tenant's share, and the peasants—tenants and freeholders alike—were taxed exhorbitantly for the privilege of working the land. They were obliged to provide hospitality for the lord and his troops. They paid taxes in lieu of military service or construction work on castles, roads, and bridges. They were taxed for the birth of a child, a marriage, or a death and were required to use the lord's mill and to pay tax on each yoke of oxen they owned. In a sense, the day laborers actually had an advantageous position since they were free men, but, not being landholders, were not taxed as the others were. They might even slip off to the city.

The decrees of the bishop of Santiago in 1113 illustrate the relatively enlightened administration of Santiago de Compostela. Many of the decrees have to do with taxes, privileges of the church, public safety, and fines. The administration of justice is spelled out, and a genuine concern is evidenced for the rights of the lower classes as well as of property owners.

"On the first day of each month the archpriests, priests, knights and peasants are to assemble to try cases and have justice administered by the archpriests and other prudent men. If the case cannot be decided by them, it shall be referred to the bishop and lay authorities of the see for their decision."

"Every Friday cases will be heard by the bishop, judges, and canons in the episcopal palace."

"Inheritances and cases concerning the church are to be tried by judges of the See of Santiago de Compostela."

"Thieves who are convicted three times are to be turned over to the lay authorities to be punished and even executed."

"To be valid, seals must be affixed before the assembly of the church or the public council."

"If a powerful man takes legal action against a poor man, he must be represented by a person of the same class as the defendant so that the judges will not be influenced by the poverty of the one and the magnificence of the other."

"Fines levied on poor people must not be so great as to deprive them of a means of livelihood."

"Houses may be seized only for robbery, murder, rape, or failure to pay the Lenten tax. Any property taken as security must be preserved intact for eight days; this includes draft animals, which shall not be worked. If the accused does not appear, the judges shall keep part of the goods, the amount depending on the gravity of the offense. If possessions are taken unjustly, twice the amount must be returned and a fine of sixty sueldos must be paid to the bishop. If the seizure was made legally, then double restitution does not have to be made."

"A man's goods are to be preserved intact for forty days after his death, and after that claims against the property and titles to it shall be settled by judges of the see and other prudent men after a full investigation."

"The possessions of anyone taken captive by the Moors must be kept intact for one full year in case the captive can be ransomed; but after a year, the goods are to be distributed according to the wishes of the family."

Public safety involved not only criminals but dangerous animals as well:

"Every Saturday except at Easter and Pentecost, the priests, knights, and peasants shall dedicate themselves to the work of hunting wolves. Every church shall supply seven iron pikes. Anyone who does not help in the hunt shall pay a fine: priests and knights, five sueldos; and peasants, one sueldo or a sheep."

The last three decrees are especially intended to insure the viability of the city and cathedral and suggest the close connection of the church, the pilgrimage, and the economic life of the town:

"Anyone who confiscates the goods of merchants, pilgrims to Rome, or pilgrims to Compostela shall make double restitution, be excommunicated, and fined."

"Clerics are exempt from paying the taxes. Abbots and clerics are not to be robbed when going to a church council or delivering the *Voto de Santiago* or the tithes."

"The measuring stone in the marketplace of Santiago de Compostela shall be the standard used for commercial transactions in the city and its surrounding territory. Anyone who does not use the standard measure shall pay a fine of sixty sueldos and shall be excommunicated until he repents." (*Historia Compostelana,* Book I, chapter 96)

The scope of the decrees shows the breadth of church power and interests. Although the pope, as Christ's vicar on earth, ruled absolutely in the spiritual realm, he delegated authority to the archbishops and abbots. Each archbishop had his bishops, canons, archdeacons and archpriests, and priests; each abbot had his priors, monks, lay brothers, and serfs. The church, like the state, exercised executive, legislative, and judicial powers and had extensive land holdings. The cathedrals and monasteries were free from secular control, and the clergy acquired large amounts of land through pious donations and wills. By the twelfth century these two parallel hierarchies—secular and ecclesiastical—were inextricably interlocked; and it was sometimes questionable whether a holding or privilege belonged to the church or to a secular lord.

The archbishop, as a feudal lord in his own right and equal to the greatest Galician nobles, ruled the city. The *Tierra de Santiago* (the land belonging to the see) as an important political entity dated back to the ninth century when the land for three miles—later, six miles—around the tomb of the Apostle was expressly given to the church. Although the charters granting the land are twelfth-century forgeries drawn up by Gelmírez to protect the see, ample evidence exists for the ninth-century origin of the *Tierra de Santiago.* The archbishop held executive, legislative, and judicial power over the area and had vicars and sheriffs for the administration of the holdings and the collection of taxes. As noted in the decrees the episcopal court met on

Tuesday and Friday, and the full local assembly on the first of each month. Although bishops and abbots, as temporal authorities, had more exemptions than lay lords, the kings usually intervened in their territories and taxed the people independently. Gelmírez made every effort to prevent this abuse in his realm; even the king had to get permission to arrest a subject there.

The archbishop had three means of controlling the nobility. First, he could force them to swear oaths which they nearly always broke as soon as it was convenient. Next, as archbishop, he could excommunicate, a terrible penalty in the Middle Ages but insufficient to stop a thoroughly evil magnate. Finally, he had his own militia whose strength formed the basis of his power.

In the cathedral canons assisted the archbishop. At the head of the chapter was the abbot, later called a prior, and under him were the dean, treasurer, and archdeacons who supervised the clergy. The canons acted as judges in the episcopal court and served the cathedral in various capacities including service at the altars.

One of Gelmírez' first acts on ascending the episcopal throne was to reorganize and reform the cathedral chapter. He increased the number of canons to seventy-two. Then he ordered the canons to shave and to dress properly in the cathedral, that is, to wear vestments, and not to wear boots and spurs in the choir. He provided a refectory because some men were actually going hungry and a dormitory for those without a private home, but he did not require them to use it. He insisted that canons have enough education to read and perform the liturgical services correctly. He introduced the study of oratory and logic into the cathedral school, and some canons were sent to France to study grammar and philosophy.

To enhance the splendor of the services, Gelmírez gained from the pope the privilege of having cardinals in the chapter. Only five other sees (three in Germany and two in France) had this honor. Thus, Santiago de Compostela had seven cardinals who had the right to wear jeweled mitres, the right to assist at Pontifical Masses, and the exclusive right of weekly service at the high altar. Cardinals did not have to be priests; Hugh, for example, became a cardinal in 1104 but was not ordained until 1113, the day before he became bishop of Oporto.

The financial organization of the church is described in the *Codex Calixtinus:*

———————————

"Each week the canons divide among themselves the offerings from the altar of St. James. To the first canon the offerings of the first week are given; the second, to the second; the third, to the third; and so on until the last. Each Sunday, traditionally, the offering is divided into three parts: the first part goes to the man in charge of the services for the week. The two other parts are combined and in turn divided into three parts: one part is given to the canons for their food; another, for construction work on the basilica; the third, to the Archbishop. But the offerings of the week from Palm Sunday to Easter are given to the poor pilgrims in the hospital of Santiago. Furthermore, if one observes the Divine law, one should at all times give a tenth part of the offering made at the altar of St. James to the poor who arrive at the hospital. For the love of God and the Apostle all the poor pilgrims ought to receive complete hospitality at the hospital on the night which follows the day of their arrival at the altar of Santiago. The sick ought to be charitably cared for until their death or complete recovery. This is done at St. Leonard's [Limoges]. All the poor who arrive there are given a meal. Furthermore, offerings which come to the altar between matins and tierce each Sunday are usually given to the lepers of the city." (*Codex Calixtinus,* Book V, chapter 10)

The church had an important economic as well as a religious and political role. The archdeacon supervised the activities of the clerics who were rectors of individual churches. As we have noted, both the bishop and the abbot held the position of lay lords; and each ruled with his chapter of canons or monks. The holdings of the archbishop of Compostela were made very complicated by the many donations of private property, including churches. A church built on private property belonged to the person who owned the property and built it. This person had the right to the rents, tithes, and offerings "voluntary, customary, and obligatory" and in turn was responsible for the maintenance of the fabric of the buildings. The builder also had the right to name the priest and was responsible for the well-being of the staff, and he had the right to transfer ownership of the church by will or gift. Thus not only did laymen own churches, but might give a bishop a church in another bishop's diocese. Gelmírez acquired as many churches as possible for the see of Santiago, for these donations of property provided the enormous wealth of Santiago. The parishes benefited as well, because the archbishops saw to it that their buildings were modernized and kept in good repair.

The role of the burghers in this organization, as we have seen, became increasingly important. Santiago de Compostela, as the seat first of a bishop and then of an archbishop and as the richest and most important trading and commercial center in the realm, was pre-eminent in the period in spite of the fact that the king usually resided in León or

101

Castile. The citizens of Compostela had their city council with some administrative authority in minor matters; but they were subject to the archbishop's laws, courts, and vicars. To insure their rights, the citizens organized into political leagues, or brotherhoods, and even defied ecclesiastical authority when they felt their rights to be threatened.

The city of Santiago de Compostela played a vital role in the economic development of the region and the kingdom. Guilds of craftsmen and merchants existed even in the twelfth century. No information about the actual organization of guilds in Compostela during this early period has survived; the first formal rules of which we learn are those of the money changers of 1289. The guilds must have resembled those of the later periods. A master and other officers elected annually had the responsibility for training and admitting candidates to membership, evaluating work, settling disputes and providing mutual aid and protection (for example, the guilds were responsible for providing appropriate funerals for their members). Widows remained in the guild and could carry on their husbands' business as long as they did not marry a member of a rival guild. Santiago de Compostela in the later Middle Ages had an unusually liberal policy toward foreigners, perhaps because the citizens were so accustomed to them in their city. Since foreign craftsmen were taken into the guilds and allowed to open shops in Compostela, the Compostelan guilds were not quite as protectionist as most; and the craftsmen seem to have been more responsive to outside influence in both techniques and taste than is usual in the period.

From the beginning—the building of the first church around the tomb of the Apostle—the building trades were important in Compostela, and masons and carpenters were in constant demand—for the building of the first church, then the monastic community, the second and third churches, and finally the present cathedral. Great buildings cannot be erected on the basis of peasants' day service. In fact, the bishop did away with the obligation to provide labor on buildings and replaced this duty with a small tax with which he could hire full-time, professional labor. And although the canon in charge of the fabric must have been grateful for the pilgrims' efforts in carrying blocks of lime from the distant quarries to the mortar works, the chapter did not rely on a "cult of carts" to erect its monumental cathedral. By 1131 the masons were given a special charter by Alfonso VII in which they were freed from military service and from paying the military exemption tax. Their homes and property were exempt even from the bishop's officials, and the Master Mason was given judicial authority over them. (Charter reproduced in López Ferreiro, Vol. IV, app. VI.)

The growth of independence experienced by the masons is typical of the changing role of the skilled craftsman in the twelfth century. We know that in 1168 the master of the shop, Master Matthew, was given a lifetime grant by the king for his work on the cathedral.

―――――――――――――

"In the name of Our Lord, Jesus Christ. Amen. It behooves His Royal Majesty to make better provision for those who are known to show faithful allegiance to him and especially to men who are forever to pay unceasing homage to the sanctuaries and holy places of God. Therefore, I, Ferdinand, by the grace of God, King of Spain, out of love for God Almighty and out of reverence for St. James, our most holy patron, as a gift, grant and concede to you, Master Matthew, who exercises the supervision and overseeing of the work of the aforesaid Apostle, at the middle of each year from my mint, money for the upkeep of St. James's amounting to two

103

marks each week, and what falls short one week let that be made up another week, so that this fund shall bring you one hundred *maravedis* a year. This grant, gift (and duty) I give to you to hold for your lifetime, so that both the work on St. James's and your own person may benefit, and let those who have witnessed this apply themselves to the aforesaid task the more zealously." (Tumbo A, cathedral archives, reproduced in López Ferreiro, Vol. IV, app. 37.)

Two marks of silver a week was a handsome sum in 1168. It was probably expected that Matthew would keep the one hundred *maravedis* for himself and pay his men with the rest. (Or the two marks were to be paid only those weeks he worked.)

Besides these artisans (whom we would call architects, sculptors, engineers, builders, and contractors) another group of citizens whose incomes were directly dependent on the cathedral arose: the *concheros* or merchants who sold the scallop-shell badges of the pilgrims to Santiago de Compostela.

"There are some shellfish in the sea near Santiago, which are commonly called *vieiras,* which have two valves like plate armor, one on each side, between which, as between the two leather reinforcements for armor, is hidden a molusk similar to an oyster. These shells look like the fingers of the hand . . . on their return the pilgrims to the sanctuary of St. James wear them on their cloaks for the glory of the Apostle and in remembrance of him; and as a symbol of the long journey, they carry them home with great joy. The type of armor with which the shell-fish protects itself symbolizes the two rules of charity with which those who wear it ought to protect themselves, that is, love God above all other and treat one's neighbor as oneself." (*Codex Calixtinus,* Book I, chapter 17)

Many pilgrims made the journey to the coast to see the spot where St. James had been brought ashore and the scene of the miracle of the horseman. They picked up shells, and natural scallop shells must have been the original badges. By the twelfth century badges were made of all kinds of materials, even silver and jet, and the vendors were organized into a guild. The business was so flourishing and the selling of "false" shells was such an abuse that by the end of the century, February 9, 1200, the archbishop fixed the number of authorized dealers at one hundred. The proceeds of twenty-eight shops were to go to the cathedral, and the remaining seventy-two were assigned to the guild which was responsible for renting licenses to their members for a thirty-year period.

Other early guilds were those of the silversmiths, including jet carvers, the money changers, and also—although they are not mentioned in early documents—the embroiderers, including the tailors. Santiago de Compostela was famous for the production of liturgical objects and vestments. The elaborateness and high quality of their work can be inferred from descriptions such as that of the furniture of the sanctuary in the *Pilgrims' Guide.* The *Historia Compostelana* mentions many fine objects produced in Compostela, including a gold chest and gold chalice sent as gifts to the pope. Vestments produced in the city were considered worthy presents, too, and were sent by the archbishop to other bishops. Jet carving was the most distinctive specialty of Compostela. The only other important medieval source of objects in this material, which was thought to have great therapeutic powers, was Whitby, in England.

The early organization of the money changers and the many references to them reminds us that money was coming into general use. In the twelfth century many financial transactions in cash are recorded, although the economy was not really based on money until the thirteenth century. The basic unit of money used in Compostela was the silver mark of about two-thirds of a pound of silver. The mark was divided into sueldos at twenty sueldos to the pound of silver. The sueldo in turn consisted of twelve dinarios or ten nummos. The typical thirteenth-century gold coin, the maravedi, must also have been in use by the twelfth century in Santiago de Compostela because the annual salary of Master Matthew was one hundred maravedis. If the price paid by the treasurer, Bernardo, for a gold chalice represents its true value and not a hard bargain driven by the treasurer (a story recorded later in this chapter), then seven maravedis were equivalent to one silver mark, and thus a maravedi was about twice as valuable as a sueldo.

It is difficult to estimate or appreciate the purchasing power of these coins. In the early twelfth century the bishop gave the king an annual grant of 100 marks and later raised this amount to 400 and, finally, 500 marks. He bought a castle for 150 marks. Twelve marks a month was allocated for the support of the community dining hall of the seventy-two canons of the cathedral. In 1136 the citizens of Compostela offered the king a bribe of 3,000 marks in an attempt to depose the archbishop. Since the king, at first, succumbed to the temptation, 3,000 marks must have been a considerable sum and the citizens of Santiago very wealthy and very determined.

Among the special rights and privileges enjoyed by the

see of Compostela—and reflected in the prosperity of the city—was the right to coin money. Normally the mint was a royal monopoly; all money was issued in the king's name because of the great financial rewards attendant to the operation of a mint and also to prevent fraud. Monasteries or lords might receive certain profits from royal mints located in their territory, but they did not have permission to coin money themselves. When the rebuilding of the Cathedral of Santiago de Compostela was begun in the late eleventh century, the bishop was given permission to coin money for the crown. Then, in 1105, Bishop Gelmírez—through persistent and relentless pressure on the king—was able to gain full control over the Compostelan mint. The king first gave verbal permission and curiously seemed unable to believe that the bishop would actually use it. Gelmírez at once took over, appointed his own director, Tandulfo, and changed the inscription on the coins. On May 14, 1107, Alfonso gave in and made a written grant, although even then he did not actually hand over the precious document to Gelmírez until a year later. The episcopal mint of Santiago de Compostela was the first in Spain under local control. The financial power—not to mention the prestige—that a mint gave to Santiago de Compostela was enormous.

The active commercial and business life in Compostela required the development of another professional group, the notaries, or lawyers. At first documents were drawn up by a scribe, and no one was officially responsible for the accuracy of their contents. By the end of the twelfth century, however, notaries drew up all public and some private documents such as contracts, loans, payment of debts, and sales. Lope Arias is the first notary we know in Compostela. The course of his career—and with it the development of the legal profession—can be seen in the documents prepared by him. In 1170, Lope signs himself *"Lupus notarius."* After 1172, the complete form is found, *"Lupus Arie Compostellanus notarius publicus et juratus confirmat."* By the end of the century the office of notary was firmly established. As their importance grew, notaries, like Lope, hired their own scribes, who seem to have been able to serve an apprenticeship and then become notaries themselves. Three of Lope's scribes became notaries. Apparently, an educated group of men—whom we would now call lawyers and businessmen—lived in Compostela and were already asserting themselves as a major force in the realm.

Santiago de Compostela had a solid economic foundation as a market town for the surrounding countryside, which —when it was not being laid waste by wars among the nobles —could claim a relatively prosperous peasantry. Although it was an essentially agricultural region, mining and quarrying were also important; and because of its Atlantic coast, fishing was another important industry. Local ordinances strictly prohibited middlemen and limited commerce and industry to a relatively simple operation of production and sales. We must always remember, though, that the enormous wealth and political power of Compostela was based on the possession of the relics of St. James; and without the tomb the city would have been just another market town.

The importance of Santiago de Compostela as a commercial center was recognized throughout the realm, as evidenced by the decision of the king to send his chalice there for sale. The chapter on "The Acquisition of a Chalice of Gold" from the *Historia Compostelana* provides an interesting reflection of religious practices, pilgrimages, and commerce:

"The treasurer of the Church of Santiago, named Bernardo, decided to go to Jerusalem for the love of God and the remission of his sins; but when everything necessary to him was ready, and he was going to begin his trip, the Archbishop—realizing that his church would suffer much harm because of his absence and that there was no doubt that the work on the church needed his supervision very much—resolved to dissuade him from this trip and having dissuaded him, to keep him home at all costs. The Archbishop advised the treasurer then that everything that had to be personally delivered at the Holy Sepulchre and other holy places near Jerusalem could be sent by faithful messengers; and, with the money which the trip would have cost, he could buy some appropriate and precious ornament for the honor and service of God and Santiago; and once he had acquired such a gift, he could deposit it in the treasury of the church on the condition that for no reason should it be taken from there, or should it be sold or given as a donation.

While the Archbishop, with the advice of the canons, was occupied with this case, it happened that King Alfonso sent to Compostela through his minister Albertino a luxurious and magnificent gold chalice—worth seven hundred maravedis—which the King had acquired from the Archbishop of Toledo on an occasion when he had found himself in need of money; and he sent it to be sold in Compostela knowing that there was no place in Spain where it could be sold at a better price. The Archbishop, on seeing such a good and precious chalice, advised the treasurer that he should buy it, for the honor of God and Santiago, in commutation of his trip, and that with it he should honor his mother, the Church of the Apostle.

The treasurer saw that the advice of the Archbishop was both good and practical and did not argue; and, happily following this advice, he bought the chalice for one hundred marks of pure silver; and with it he enriched his church, in accordance with the advice of the Archbishop and the canons. Having done that, he was absolved of all his sins in a meeting of the full chapter just as those who make the effort to go to Jerusalem were accustomed to be absolved; for the remission of his sins he dedicated himself to the organization and implementation of the work on the Church of Santiago." (*Historia Compostelana,* Book III, chapter 8)

The great medieval fairs were usually held at the time of the major religious celebrations of the city. The two feasts of St. James, July 25 and December 30, should have been the most important fairs in Compostela. These dates, falling as they did in midwinter and midsummer, were the worst possible times from the point of view of the merchants and the pilgrims. It was only sensible to travel when the mountain passes were free of snow and when the traveler could avoid the bitter cold of winter and the scorching sun of summer on the Spanish plateau. Thus, spring and fall were the periods of the greatest influx of pilgrims and the most commercial activity; and the important fairs were held at Easter and at the Feast of St. Michael in the fall.

In connection with these fairs, merchants had to be permitted passage to the city with their goods; and the abuse of travelers had to be dealt with firmly for the good of the city. An instance of abuse involved the castle warden of San Pelayo de Luto, who not only collected a royal toll but often injured the merchants and stole their goods, even their clothes. Indeed, the legal tolls and taxes on movement of goods and market transactions were among the greatest impediments to the development of commerce and a better standard of living in the Middle Ages. Recognizing this fact, Gelmírez in 1095 convinced the count of Galicia to abolish the toll at San Pelayo de Luto; and the count decreed that no one was to confiscate the goods of merchants or residents of Compostela, that complaints by merchants were to be heard by the bishop and chapter, and that offenders were to be fined and required to make double restitution to be divided between the bishop and the victim.

Two documents provide us with a remarkably clear picture of the economic life of Santiago de Compostela in the twelfth century. The first is the decree of 1133 establishing local ordinances for the control of prices and measurements in the city as recorded in the *Historia Compostelana.* The second is a portion of a sermon against the evils of the businessmen of Compostela supposedly preached by Pope Calixtus II but probably written by the author of the *Pilgrims' Guide.*

———————

"This is the decree which the canons of St. James the Apostle, and the judges and the citizens of Compostela, with the authorization and confirmation of the King, don Alfonso, and the Archbishop, don Diego, established as obligatory, abolishing all the bad ordinances and establishing good ones which are always to be preserved. They are as follows:

For good Castela wine brought into the city no less than eight *quartas* [about nine gallons] are to be given for each mark. For other good wine which is brought by boat, no less than twelve *quartas* are to be given for a mark. He who buys it may take for himself one *quarta* for each mark and sell the rest unadulterated, faithfully observing the measure prescribed by the council. . . . A peasant or citizen who brings in cider should sell it himself without any adulteration and should give four full cups [a Galician cup was equivalent to a *quarta*] measured by the standard of the measuring cask of Fernando Velázquez or by other similar ones; for good cider in casks in this city, he should give three cups for a nummo [one-tenth of a sueldo]. Let no one presume to establish a tavern for the sale of cider, whether it is in casks or in pitchers.

"No one is to buy fish, meat, shellfish, octopus, lobsters, lamprey eels, kid, bread, or fruit to make a profit by reselling, but only so that he may eat. Merchants of this city who go to the seashore and to the bays for any kind of fish are not to sell it to a peddler, unless he sells it publicly to both citizens and foreigners. Likewise, those who go about the country buying cattle, hogs, and other meats are not to sell them to other peddlers but to the citizens or butchers; and the butchers are to buy them under supervision of the council, butcher them by day in the marketplace, and sell them without fraud at the lawful weight laid down by the council according to ancient custom. This does not apply to oxen, which we do not permit to be slaughtered, except for old oxen and those unfit for the plow.

"We add also that no one shall dare to buy horses, mares, oxen and calves from sheriffs, thieves, or robbers or from any unknown person who does not give security. Cheese and butter are to be sold by weight according to ancient custom.

"As for fish, we also declare that no less than five large or ten small sea breams or mullets are to be sold for a nummo. A large eel is to be sold for a denario, a large octopus for two denarios and a medium one, for one; both fresh and salted hake are to be sold at three for a denario; no less than fifty large oysters, for one denario; no less than sixty sardines, for one; conger eels of eight palms, at seven denarios, and good ones of medium size, at no more than three; lampreys, at no more than three.

"A big male goat, at no more than ten nummos; a good lamb with white hide, at no more than six denarios; a good one skinned, for three nummos; a hen, a *maraticam,* and a partridge, for one nummo each; a good rabbit, for two nummos; no less than thirty eggs are to be given for a nummo. A good kid with the skin is to be sold for no more than three nummos; a good goose, at no more than four nummos, an excellent sheep, at no more than eight nummos.

"Women bakers who have houses or property for carrying out their work are to buy at the true rate and bake good, salted, clean bread, without fraud, at one nummo or mealia [that is, half a nummo] according to the weight prescribed for them by the council; and after having taken out their taxes, let them earn no more than four nummos. Innkeepers, minters, money changers and citizens are not to have false marks, pounds, or weights; and especially innkeepers are not to have women bakers in or out of their houses. Wax, pepper, cumin seeds, and incense are to be sold by true pounds.

"Smiths are to sell only the best shoes for horses and mules at no more than two nummos a pair; those that are less good for three mealia; a good ax should not cost more than eight nummos; a good hoe, no more than four; the best plowshare should be three; a less good one, two; a reaping hook, one nummo and a sickle for use among the rocks, one mealia.

"As for footwear, the best laced goatskin boots should be sold without fraud for no more than eighteen nummos; good boots for no more than two sueldos; the best women's shoes for no more than twelve nummos; good workmen's shoes of oxhide for no more than five nummos; the rest, for four or three according to their value; the best wooden shoes for no more than three nummos; the rest, for one nummo or three obolos or two nummos according to their value;

the best goatskin shoes with laces for no more than twelve nummos. . . .

"Innkeepers are not to go beyond the Miño in buying or selling the above-mentioned things. No one is to do violence or fraud to the seller; and by violence is meant injustice. And both buyers and sellers who act contrary to this decree are to pay five sueldos; sellers are to be punished by whipping and are to lose their business. We declare and confirm that anyone publicly guilty of violating these decrees is not to be received into any house or private property.

"The entire council shall select suitable men; three to establish the measure for wine, namely Pelayo Astráriz, with Pelayo Albo, Alvito Candanátiz, and Esteban Paláez; three to inspect bread, Froilan Rosende, Miguel Martínez, and Arias Guntádiz, who are to supervise the evaluation and the weighing of bread. Likewise for meat, Pelayo Astráriz, Fernando Justílaz, Juan Arias, and Pelayo Viliúlfiz; and following their evaluation we shall establish the weight and the stone [weight] for the pork and beef; and even when it may be necessary to raise or lower prices, they shall not be increased or decreased without the consent, order, and judgment of the canons, judges, citizens, and vicar of the city.

"Enacted Era 1171 [that is, 1133], May 7."*(Historia Compostelana,* Book III, chapter 33)

———————

The prices quoted are generally in denarios or nummos. The prices, are, of course, interesting on a comparative basis and as an indication of the preferences and availability of foodstuffs in Santiago. In the fields around Santiago grew rye, barley, oats, and millet; however, wheat was a luxury imported from Castile especially for the making of wafers for the church. Both fresh and dried chestnuts are also mentioned in documents, as are apples, cherries, pears, and nuts. Monasteries had extensive orchards; and one of the first activities undertaken in a new or re-established house was the planting of trees of all kinds, especially apples. Cider was so much cheaper than wine that we may assume that the peasants and citizenry drank it as their usual beverage. People preferred wine, for the many references to both beverages invariably deprecate cider. Donations of wine to the cathedral chapter for the canons are frequent. Not everyone ate well, even in the cathedral chapter. One of Bishop Gelmírez' reforms—as soon as he assumed the see—was to insure that all the canons were given an equal ration of bread and wine.

Perhaps one of the best indications of business practice in the twelfth century is to be found in the sermon of Pope Calixtus. The fraudulent prices mentioned come from the same period as the official price list and provide an interesting comparison.

"Moreover, what is there to say about the wicked innkeepers who cheat the pilgrims with so many deceptions? . . . Those who treat people badly in the inns on the road to Santiago, exploiting the pilgrims with innumerable ruses, are condemned. Some innkeepers go to meet the pilgrims at the entrances of the cities, kissing them as if they were relatives arriving from distant lands. What else do they do? Lodging them in their houses, they promise them only good but do evil. To whom are they similar except to the traitor Judas who betrayed the Lord with a kiss? They give the pilgrims a sample of good wine and sell them a poor one. Others substitute cider for wine; others sell adulterated wine instead of good wine. Others sell fish or meat cooked two or three days earlier, making the pilgrims sick. Others show the pilgrim a large measure; and if they can, sell to them with a small one. Some have false measures for the wine and the oats, which appear large on the outside but are shallow and narrow on the inside, that is, they have been hollowed out only a little way. . . . There are those who bring wine from the barrel. and if they are able, put water in the glass beforehand. Others promise comfortable beds and provide detestable ones. Others, when more guests come, turn away the first after having received payment. The evil innkeeper does not give the pilgrims a good bed unless they give him supper or some money. If the pilgrim's coins are worth two coins in the city where he wants to eat, the wicked innkeeper gives him only an *obolo* [one-fourth their true value]. The evil innkeeper gives a lot of good wine to his guests in order to make them drunk; and when they are asleep, he steals their purses or satchels or other belongings. The evil innkeeper even gives them poisoned drinks in order to steal their possessions.

"Also going to the torture of the damned are the fiends who make two compartments in a wine barrel and put a different kind of wine in each. They offer a sample of the better wine, and then after dinner they bring poor wine drawn from the second compartment. . . . And what should one say about the servant who, at the orders of the landlord, throws out the water which is in the house so that the thirsty pilgrims, having no water to drink at night, buy wine from the landlord? And what should one say of the maid who steals the oats and the rye from the mangers with the consent of the landlord? We pronounce anathema against them. The maids in the inns on the road of Santiago who, for shameful motives, and to gain money at the instigation of the devil, go to the beds of the pilgrims are completely worthy of condemnation. The prostitutes who for these same motives come out to meet the pilgrims in mountainous regions between

Puerto Marín and Palas de Rey not only should be excommunicated but also ought to be stripped, taken, and shamed, their noses cut off, and exposed to public derision. The women usually present themselves to single men. In so many ways, brothers, does the devil set his fiendish nets and open the way to perdition to the pilgrims that I am sick describing them.

"On the other hand, what is there to say about the evil innkeepers who out of avarice keep the money of the pilgrims who die in their inns, which ought to be given as offerings to the poor and to the clerics? The evil innkeepers of the city of Santiago give their lodgers the first meal free and only sell them candles and beeswax. Oh, false charity! Oh, false piety! Oh, generosity filled with deception! If the owner of the house has twelve pilgrims on a particular date and for the first meal gives them meat or fish which costs eight denarios in the city; the deceiving man makes a gift of it; but then he brings twelve candles, each one of which is sold in the market for four denarios, and he sells them for six sueldos. He cheats each one by six denarios. . . . What more is there to say? The meat and fish which he gave the pilgrims to eat was worth eight denarios, but in reality he has fraudulently sold the food to them and overcharged by two sueldos. Oh, nefarious merchant! Oh, detestable lucre! . . .

"Some, cleverly looking ahead, send a servant from the city of Santiago to Puerto Marín to meet the pilgrims so that they can talk with them in this manner: 'My brothers and friends, I am from the city of Santiago, and I did not come here in search of guests, but I am in this city to care for my master's sick mule; go then to his house and tell him that his mule will soon be well, and stay there, because for my sake, when you tell him this good news, he will treat you well.' And when they arrive there they find everything bad.

"Another goes to Barbadelo or to Tricastela to meet the pilgrims; and after wishing them health and talking cleverly of other things, he says to them: 'My brothers traveling to Santiago, I am a rich citizen of that city, and I have not come here to find lodgers but rather to talk with my brother who lives in this city; so if you want a good lodging in Santiago, take lodging in my house, and tell my wife and my family to treat you well, for my sake; I will give you a token to show them.' Thus with false words he gives one pilgrim his knife, another his hat, another his gloves as tokens and sends them to his house. When they arrive at the man's house and lodge there, after having fed them, the mistress of the house sells them a candle which is worth four denarios for eight or ten. In this way the pilgrims to Santiago are cheated by the innkeeper. . . . And if the pilgrim has coins to change, this innkeeper, wanting to get the commission, gets him to give twenty of his coins in exchange for twelve local coins in spite of the fact that they are worth about sixteen. Thus the evil innkeepers cheat the pilgrims and are to be condemned.

"The guards who look after the altars of the basilica of Santiago—St. Gil, St. Leonardo, St. Martin of Tours, and St. Peter in Rome—are accomplices of the landlords who make a profit by taking the pilgrims to the altars and advising them to leave their offerings there, so that the innkeeper receives a commission from the guards who also fraudulently get their share. And what should one say about the guard who after having already stolen part of the offerings at the altar, still demands his portion of the remainder from the rectors of the altar and the church?

"The pilgrims must take special precautions against certain swindlers commonly called *cinnatores* who lie in ambush along the roads. Some change money with counterfeit coins; others steal while making the exchange, others pretend to sell thongs, belts, cords, gloves, beeswax, or something else, pretending to give a low price. And while one shows the goods to the pilgrim, the other thief hides the pilgrim's genuine money in his sleeve and substitutes counterfeit coins. Another throws an ounce of false gold on the road where the pilgrims will be passing; and when they come upon it, he leans down and picks it up from the ground to look at. And then since the pilgrims have found it with him, he wants to divide the profits; but the clever swindler, pretending to be poor, sells his share, which is worth only a pin, dearly for four or five sueldos of true gold. Also one must warn the pilgrims against some evil innkeepers who put their rings or their silver seals in the saddlebags or satchels of the lodgers when they are sleeping at night; and when the pilgrims leave the inn and are a mile away, the innkeepers pursue them, and with this fraudulent pretext the innkeepers rob them. . . . [False clerics and beggars are then described]

". . . Every iniquity and every deception flourishes on the roads of the saints. And what shall I say about the false bankers whom the vulgar call money changers? . . . If a mark of pure silver is worth thirty sueldos, the money changer will give only twenty for it. The wily money changer has different weights, large and small. He buys the silver with the larger weight and sells it with the smaller. He raises the value of his gold, silver, and jewels and lowers that of others. He sells dearly and buys cheaply. If he can, he cheats others, but he looks after himself carefully. He weighs every coin for himself in a scale called a *trebuqueto* and sells to others the heaviest at a higher price; or he recasts it in the foundry with different silver. He maliciously breaks large coins with a pair of tongs and beats them out so that they appear large. Oh, what frauds he commits a thousand and one times!

"What does that evil man do? A ring, a chalice, or a

candlestick or any other object of silver-plated bronze he sells more dearly as pure silver to the ignorant if he can. In the same way, he fraudulently sells a gilt object as gold. He sells, if he can, his marks of silver or talents of gold at a higher price, as assayed silver and gold, although they are not assayed; and on the other hand, he buys those of others at a lower price as if they were not assayed, although they are. If the mark or talent of the pilgrim is worth four denarios less than the legal weight requires, he buys it and discounts twelve. If the gold or silver of that banker is in a ring, or a vase, or a candlestick, or a bridle, or any other object, he sells it as pure gold, although it is not, and also charges for the workmanship in the piece. And if the pilgrim tries to sell the same piece, he will buy it only as unassayed gold or silver. The same thing is done with stones which are not precious or counterfeit stones similar to precious stones; he sells them to the unwary as very precious stones. He commits these and other villainies, thus bringing himself to the infernal snare without noticing it; and catching himself with his own tricks and falling into his own trap. . . .

"And what shall we say of the cheating apothecary? Some keep herbs for such a long time that they spoil, and then they sell them as good. Others sell fake spices as precious ones. Some sprinkle the pepper with water so that it weighs more in the scale. Others add roasted juniper berries or black sand to it; others mix in *barbara glisce,* similar to alum; others mix resin from the fir or pine with the incense; there are those who mix in earth when they sell pigments; others sell verdigris for azure to the ignorant; others, lead oxide instead of vermillion; others mix lead oxide with vermillion; others sprinkle the azure with water so that it weighs more. In the same way the other colors and spices are adulterated with things similar in appearance to them.

"The doctors do the same thing. They are not afraid wickedly to adulterate medicinal honey, drugs, sirups, and other antidotes with other ingredients. They mix good things with bad ones and sell the adulterated preparations as herbs of great value.

"And what is there to say about fraudulent businessmen? Some buy cloth with a long measuring stick and sell it with a short one; others keep it so long it rots, in spite of which they sell it as of good quality; some sell the thongs, wild animal skins, belts, gloves, and other objects at a higher price to pilgrims than to their neighbors; others frequently swear falsely for the slightest reason, for which they are to be condemned; others stretch out the new cloth they have to sell with their hands to make it longer and wider than it should be; others sell thongs of sheep or pig skin or horsehide as if they were deerskin; the belts, purses, scabbards of pigskin or sheepskin they fraudulently sell to the unwary as if they were deerskin. Oh, deceitful avarice! There are those who insist that their servants learn these tricks and send them to Le Puy, St. Gilles, Tours, Plasencia, Lucca, Rome, Bari, and Barletta because in these cities there are schools for all kinds of trickery.

"Oh you false innkeepers, cheating bankers, and wicked merchants, convert to the Lord our God, put aside your evils, your avarice, throw out your wicked deceptions! What will you say at the Last Judgment when you see all those whom you have cheated accusing you before God?" (*Codex Calixtinus,* Book I, chapter 17)

Life in Santiago de Compostela was not as hazardous for the resident as for the gullible pilgrim; although like other medieval cities, Compostela might seem crowded and poor to us today. Narrow streets opened into squares named for the occupations of the inhabitants: the bakers' or butchers' square, the street of the money changers or jet workers. Most houses had only one or two stories. On the ground floor were shops, workrooms, and a courtyard with stable. In an inn, or if the house were very large, a second or even third story with the main living area was corbeled out over the street, giving a little more interior space. Travelers were housed everywhere when the city was crowded.

Rooms in twelfth-century dwellings were not designed for specific purposes, with the exception of the kitchen and stable. The kitchen consisted of a room with a large hearth on which food was prepared by roasting on spits or boiling in cauldrons and kettles. The function of other rooms was determined by the contents of the large chests which were used both for storage and as seats. Trestle tables, folding stools, chests, and beds were the essential items of furniture, along with cooking utensils, blankets, and wall and bed hangings and pillows. The prized possessions of a household can be learned from twelfth-century wills. Juan Froilaz in 1170 left cooking utensils, chests, cups, and a bed with four pillows. Sheets and towels are also mentioned in wills, and rich fabrics were especially prized in the twelfth century. Although no early fabrics survive in Compostela, enough are preserved in the treasuries of other churches for us to gain a good idea of the intricacy of their patterns, the brilliance of the colors, and the exquisite refinement of the spinning and weaving techniques. The townspeople appreciated a fine piece of cloth; and clothing, wall hangings, sheets, and towels were handed down from generation to generation.

Christian cities lacked the facilities for public health and sanitation found in Moorish cities. Public latrines were the rule only in larger cities. Community fountains were numerous in Santiago, which because of its size and large number

122

of monastic establishments and inns had suffered from an acute shortage of water until the aqueduct and fountain in the Paraiso were built.

Compostela was one of the large medical centers of the Middle Ages. Because of the necessity of caring for the pilgrims, and perhaps under some influence from contacts with the Moors, an unusual emphasis was placed on public health. Facilities for the care of pilgrims were provided in the monasteries and also in a large public hospital supported by the cathedral chapter. Not only did pilgrims fall sick along the road, but many of those making the journey were doing so in the hope of a miraculous cure, and the trip could only have made the majority of them much worse. A special funeral chapel and cemetery for pilgrims was located northwest of the cathedral.

Physical ailments were attended to by the monks and priests, and the rise of the lay doctor was slow. A medical school was not founded in Christian Spain until the thirteenth century, in Palencia; however, the study and practice of medicine flourished in the Moorish kingdoms. One of the leading medical schools of Europe was in Córdoba, where anatomy, surgery, and pharmacy were taught. The Moors inherited the scientific knowledge of the Greeks, and it was primarily from Moorish Spain that the ancient medicine was transmitted to the investigators of the Renaissance. Good Christians were, of course, prohibited from consulting the infidels, but in the throes of sickness many turned to every possible source, and the Moors and Jews must have been secretly consulted.

The patient was treated with baths, enemas, blood-letting, and a variety of medicines. Medieval pharmacology is a fascinating combination of folk wisdom and fantasy. Most intriguing today is the use of precious stones, pearls, coral, silver, and gold as healing agents. Their medical use was linked to astrology; the heavenly bodies with which they were associated and which it was thought controlled man could be activated by their presence.

Medicines derived from plants were more likely to be helpful, and the use of the plant was often tied to its religious significance. The medicinal properties of the lily, for example, are described in the *Codex Calixtinus.*

―――――――――――

"Santiago is represented by the lily that dies in the winter and in the summer produces white perfumed flowers, because Santiago suffered the afflictions of martyrdom in this world in the winter season and in the happy summer season through the merit of his good works, he is in the luxuriance of eternally flowering Paradise before God. . . . The medicinal virtues of the lily are described by Dioscorides, Master of Medicine: . . . The properties of the lily, they say, soften the hardness of the bodily nerves; thus Santiago is filled with the strength of the Holy Ghost by the absolutions which he made, reducing the strength of the sins of the souls and loosening the chains of vice. The boiled leaves of the lily are beneficial for parts of the body attacked by fever because the good works of Santiago and his divine words are profitable to mankind encompassed by the flames of vice. The leaves of the lily cure serpent bites in the body, thus Santiago with his preaching and absolutions counteracted the traps laid by the devil in the souls of the sinners. Just as the serpent with poison in his fangs stabs the flesh of many, the devil attacks the mind with evil suggestions. The juice of the lily cures chronic wounds; Santiago cures the errors of the Old Law and the rotting wounds of sin by his mellifluous preaching and divine absolutions. The root of the lily roasted and mixed with oil is useful for burns and helps menstrual purging; thus the Apostolic faith mixed with the fire of the Holy Ghost and the oil of mercy and piety and pervading the soul through divine preaching eases mankind encompassed by the flames of vice; and with the water of baptism he cleanses man of sin. The fact that the seed of the lily placed in a drink brings on menstruation and cures snake bite has the same meaning as the root and the flower. The fact that it hastens childbirth signifies the virginal chastity of the Blessed Mary which should be believed by the faithful." (*Codex Calixtinus,* Book I, chapter 17)

One of the most difficult medical problems was the man or woman who was bewitched (probably actually suffering from epilepsy or psychological disturbances). These cures were left in the hands of the church, and attempts were made to exorcise the devil. Undoubtedly many illnesses of psychological nature could respond favorably to the cure, much as faith healing of our own times.

An early form of public welfare or relief was established at Santiago, and again, its early appearance was due to the special needs of the pilgrimage. Any pilgrim could have free room and board for three days in the hospital and inn built by the church. The cathedral chapter also provided clothes, probably just a tunic and perhaps a cloak and sandals, for threadbare and poverty-stricken pilgrims. The *Historia Compostelana* describes the ritual of leaving the pilgrims' rags in the cathedral to be burned later, while the pilgrim was given new clothing. A portion of the offering at the high altar and all the offerings at the high altar during Holy Week were reserved for the care of pilgrims.

The church and the state also combined to protect the

pilgrims and citizenry through the establishment of the military orders to act as a police force for northern Spain. The church issued passes of safe conduct for travelers and instituted a Peace of God. Still, the church had to rely on oaths and on the threat of excommunication to enforce its laws. Even the direst threats were not enough to keep the nobles under control, as for example in the case of the robbery of the English merchants. The church's concern for the safety of pilgrims and merchants was not entirely a reflection of Christian charity; it had a sound practical basis. It was very important to the economic life of the see, the city, and all Galicia that people be able to travel freely and safely; for the wealth of the church depended on the offerings of the pilgrims and the business that they and the merchants brought. The lists of gifts by the bishop, Gelmírez, to the king or the pope or even to other prelates in the *Historia Compostelana* indicate the immense wealth of the see and the city.

In Santiago de Compostela men from all walks of life were to be seen: the clerics, the tradesmen of the town, and the peasants bringing in their produce to market; and because of the international scope of the pilgrimage, the entire range of the social hierarchy, king and count to beggar, could be seen, especially in the spring and fall. The streets of the city must have had a very motley appearance and a very tattered look as well, for even the wealthy pilgrim must have been weary and worn after such a trip. Pilgrims were advised to travel light, to wear heavy shoes, a heavy cloak, and hood or hat to protect them from the weather. Thus the throngs of laymen would have appeared somber and rustic regardless of their position and wardrobe at home. The ordinary man wore a tunic and cloak, and sheepskin capes are mentioned in wills. Browns and grays and homespuns must have dominated the scene, against which the regalia of the clergy would have shown splendidly on feast days. When possible the nobility dressed brilliantly in cloth woven by the Moors or under the influence of Moorish taste. Fragments of fabrics show elaborate repeated geometric patterns in red, green, and yellow. Cloth with gold and silver thread is also mentioned. Countess María Fernández had a gold and silver dress bordered in sable from northern Europe and a silver-plated harness for her mule. The most fashionable headdresses came from the French town of Estella in Navarre. Luxurious gilded shoes with pointed toes made by the Moors were in great demand, and Gelmírez prohibited his canons from wearing them.

Recreation consisted of athletic contests, feasts, and religious festivals. Athletic ability was required for sheer survival in the twelfth century at every level of society. Athletic contests were in effect games of war: the upper classes competed in passages of arms and horsemanship; and the lower classes in their skill with sticks and clubs, or in running and jumping. Early forms of football and baseball were played, and pictures of young men playing a game with a bat and ball appear in thirteenth century hymns in praise of the Virgin Mary. Hunting, too, was not only a sport but preparation for fighting and maintenance of a food supply. Game is not mentioned in the Compostelana price lists because it was reserved for the nobles' sport and for their consumption.

Feasting, whether carousing or banqueting, then as now, was a popular form of entertainment. Descriptions of banquets rarely are explicit in their mention of food, although one is recorded in which bread, wine, capon, kid, and pork were served. Our best and most unusual record of a banquet is a visual one: the sculpture of the banqueting hall of the archbishop's palace. There we see the benediction, servants bringing covered vessels, pitchers of wine and cider, and large circular loaves of bread, and basins, ewers, and towels for hand washing. Throughout the banquet entertainment was provided by musicians, jugglers, and animal trainers. Other diversions included acrobatic and animal acts rather like a circus, and song and poetry recitals whose themes ranged from bawdy to epic. The elegant poetry of courtly love might appeal to the upper classes, and everyone enjoyed the stories of Charlemagne and the Cid. The exploits of heroes, such as the Cid, were current events; and the minstrels traveling along the road were both newsmen and poets.

The most spectacular recreation was provided by the church. The solemn festivities, the procession, and the elaborate staging of the mass took the place of theater, cinema, and concert hall for the man of the Middle Ages. A great feast day in the church was a pageant of major proportions. The vestments of the clergy, the wardrobe of the great nobles, the king, and his retinue must have shown forth in spectacular grandeur.

The description of the procession on the feast of the Translation of St. James tells us more of the theatrically dazzling effect of the religious ritual. On the feast of the Translation, December 30, the king, Alfonso VI, was accustomed to make an offering of twelve marks of silver and twelve talents of gold on the high altar in honor of the twelve Apostles. He also paid and made presents to his knights and gave them new clothes of silk. He knighted the squires, and then held a great feast in the palace to which the entire populace, even the poorest, was invited. The beginning of the feast was announced by heralds blowing their trumpets:

"Then vested with the symbols of royalty and surrounded by squadrons of knights and different orders of commanders and counts, he [the king] marched in a procession around the basilica of Santiago according to the royal ceremony for festivals.

"The admirable silver scepter of the Spanish empire which the venerable king carried in his hands was brilliant, encrusted with golden flowers of various workmanship and with all sorts of precious stones. The diadem of gold with which the all-powerful king was crowned in honor of the Apostle was embellished with enameled flowers, niello, all kinds of precious stones, and brilliant images of animals and birds. The double-edged sword which was carried unsheathed in front of the king shone with its gilded flowers and its brilliant inscription, its golden pommel and its silver cross.

"In front of him the bishop of Santiago marched in a dignified manner wearing pontifical vestments, crowned with a white mitre, shod with gilded sandals, adorned with his golden ring, wearing white gloves, carrying the pontifical staff of ivory and surrounded by the other bishops.

"Also the clergy who advanced in front of him were decked in venerable ornaments, the copes of silk with which the seventy-two Compostelan canons were vested admirably worked with precious stones, silver brooches, golden flowers, and magnificent fringes everywhere. Some were vested with silk dalmatics decorated from the shoulders downward with golden-embroidered bands of cloth of marvellous beauty. Others were also adorned with golden necklaces encrusted with every kind of precious stone; and they decked themselves luxuriously with bands embroidered with gold, with the very richest mitres, beautiful sandals, golden belts, stoles embroidered in gold, and maniples embroidered with pearls.

"What else? The clerics of the choir were exquisitely ornamented with every sort of precious stone and with a great abundance of gold and silver. Some carried candlesticks in their hands; others, censers of silver; these, gilded crosses; those, cloths textured with gold and embellished with all sorts of precious stones; some, boxes filled with the relics of many saints; others, phylacteris; finally, others, gold or ivory batons to be used to direct the singers, the tips of which were ornamented with an onyx, a beryl, a sapphire, a carbuncle, an emerald, or some other precious stone. On carts of silver others carried two tables of gilded silver on which the devoted public put lighted beeswax candles.

"These clerics were followed by the devoted people; that is to say, the knights, governors, grandees, nobles, and both native and foreign counts dressed in gala clothes. The choirs of venerable women following them were dressed and adorned with gilded laced shoes, and with furs of marten, sable, ermine, and fox; with silk brials, gray pelisses, mantles which were scarlet outside and variegated inside, with coronets of gold, necklaces, hairpins, bracelets, earrings in their ears, chains, rings, pearls, mirrors, girdles of gold, belts of silk, veils, bows, headdresses; their braids tied with threads of gold and other varieties of dresses." (*Codex Calixtinus,* Book I, chapter 17)

VI.
Cultural Life:
The Arts and Humanities

Santiago de Compostela flourished as a center of arts and learning in the twelfth century. Called the Christian Mecca by Moorish chroniclers, the city was also a "Mecca" for builders, sculptors, scribes, poets, and musicians. Education for both clergy and laymen was encouraged, and talented youths found ample opportunity to study under the protection of the church. Cultural life centered around the cathedral, and the archbishop and chapter were great patrons of the arts. As one might assume from its political history, the "golden age" of the city of Compostela in the twelfth century had two phases: the first at the beginning of the century under the inspiration of Diego Gelmírez, and the second during the reign of Pedro Suárez in the last third of the century.

Gelmírez, as we have seen, was an enthusiastic builder. Not only did he almost finish the cathedral fabric, but he rebuilt churches and monasteries, hospitals and bridges throughout his see, constructed two episcopal palaces, and rebuilt castles and palaces in the Tierra de Santiago. Under his sponsorship the architecture of Galicia changed from the simple Asturian style to a cosmopolitan Romanesque style characterized by the use of fine ashlar masonry, vaulting

131

(although secular buildings and rural churches were still usually wooden-roofed), excellent proportions, effective planning based on the needs of the pilgrimage as well as the permanent community, and finally, whenever possible, monumental architectural sculpture and painting.

At the head of Gelmírez' artistic enterprises was the cathedral treasurer, Bernardo, a man of many talents. Bernardo was first of all an administrator, lawyer, and business executive of great ability. Not only was he a canon and treasurer of the cathedral, but later he was chancellor of the Kingdom of León. He organized the archives of the cathedral and prepared the collection of documents, of which *Tumbo A,* with its invaluable records and exquisite paintings, still exists. He was also a scholar, scribe, and painter; a mechanic, architect, and engineer. He supervised the construction of the cathedral and also of the aqueduct and fountain in the market square. Of course, the actual work was delegated to the Master Mason and his shop; however, the canon in charge of works was well versed in the techniques as well as the aesthetics of building.

The Cathedral of Santiago de Compostela was one of the revolutionary new structures in the Romanesque style. Huge in comparison with the surrounding buildings, it was literally built around the old basilica of Alfonso II and incorporated the latest innovations in structure, planning, safety, and efficiency. Of elegantly tall proportions with arcades and galleries, the building was vaulted throughout with ribbed barrel vaults over the high nave, groined vaults over the aisles, and half-barrel vaults over the galleries; but in spite of the massiveness of the stonework the cathedral was originally well lighted. Planned to handle thousands of pilgrims in a reasonable, orderly manner, the church was one of the first to take full advantage of the system of ambulatory and radiating chapels as well as aisled transepts with additional chapels, and a full circuit of the gallery with chapels there as well. The cathedral set the standard for excellence in architecture in Christian Spain.

The sculpture of the cathedral is one of the most impressive programs in western Europe in the twelfth century. Throughout the cathedral the capitals of columns and half-columns were carved with foliage, based on Roman Corinthean capitals, and with men, beasts, and interlaces. The juxtaposition of marble and granite provided a contrast in color and texture, and spiral columns of marble had rosettes, vines, or figures in interlaces, or arcades enlivening their surface. Of greatest importance are the three great sculptured portals on the north and south transepts and the west façade. These portals are described in the *Pilgrims' Guide* and have already been discussed in chapter III above.

The distinctive style of the early sculpture at Santiago de Compostela recurs in buildings along the pilgrimage road in Spain and southern France, most notably in León, Jaca, Toulouse, and Conques. The marked similarity of these sculptures led Arthur Kingsley Porter to propose his theory of a common "pilgrimage style" created by traveling masons or even a single traveling shop. Porter undoubtedly over-emphasized his position, and his opponents over-reacted to his theories. Today it seems obvious that the major monuments are really contemporary, and the style was developed simultaneously on both sides of the Pyrenees. Churchmen were well aware of what was happening in other lands. We need only remind ourselves of Gelmírez' trips through southern France to Cluny and Rome at the very time the great Romanesque buildings were under construction. Masons, too, moved with greater freedom than was usual in the period, following the demand for skilled labor on various construction projects.

This pilgrimage style in sculpture is remarkable for its physical and psychological realism in an age when the visual arts were notably abstract. Men, animals, and foliage were represented with a concern for their tangible, corporeal existence which led to a style remarkable for its insistence on three dimensional qualities and relatively accurate—although stocky—proportions. Even some details of anatomy—for example, knee joints or rib cages—were observed and represented. Faces and gestures were given a human quality quite beyond usual twelfth-century work. The impression that the artist actually looked at his surroundings rather than relying on models constantly forces itself upon the spectator. In this striving for corporeality, the figures are often excessively heavy, even bulbous, in marked contrast to the elegant, nervous, linear forms seen in contemporary work in Burgundy.

This sense of three dimensionality and of realism was the product of a combination of several influences. The sculptors had classical models to which they might refer in the still extant Roman art of southern France and Spain. Furthermore, monumental stone sculpture in Spain seems to have been influenced far more by the three-dimensional quality of the Spanish ivory carver than by the more linear and two-dimensional work of the manuscript illuminator. Sculpture in Santiago de Compostela, and in León and Jaca, often seems an enlargement and translation into stone of the tenth- and eleventh-century ivories. In short, the presence of extensive Roman remains, the importance of Spain as a center of ivory carving, combined with skill of Moorish craftsmen in the peninsula and the continuity of a tradition of stonework throughout the early Middle Ages, leads to a supposition that the style of the pilgrimage road could have been formed in Santiago de Compostela as easily as in Toulouse.

The incipient humanism of the sculpture of Santiago de Compostela may have been as influenced by the demands of the pilgrimage as was the architecture. Just as the church had to accommodate the special needs of the pilgrims, so did the sculpture have a function somewhat different from the sculpture of the monastic church or cloister. Both architecture and sculpture were commissioned by men with an essentially worldly, practical, businesslike point of view. In architecture, traffic-planning and durability were emphasized; in sculpture, Christian propaganda and the pilgrimage. Sculpture was designed for immediacy of impact. A story was told clearly and simply, and was relevant to the experience of the pilgrim or to the common body of folklore and tradition, the popular knowledge of the twelfth century. If a theme seems esoteric today, it is only because we have forgotten the tale, homily, or proverb on which it was based. The sculpture was not designed for daily contemplation, to inspire the meditations of monks, nor was it the adornment of a reliquary-like palace for God; it was meant to be seen by a traveler once or twice in his lifetime, to impress him vividly with the power and majesty of Christ and the Apostle Santiago, to make him feel that the long journey had been worth while, and to loosen his purse strings. The richness of the church permitted the execution of an elaborate, large-scale program of sculpture which met these criteria admirably.

Whether the original program of sculpture for the cathedral was ever completed is doubtful. The *Pilgrims' Guide* leaves some question because of its rather sketchy treatment of the west façade. Certainly the west façade was under construction, the iconographic program drawn up, and some sculpture finished in the shop. If it was not completed before the rebellion of 1136, it seems unlikely that the portal would have been finished during the chaotic twenty-year period that followed the death of Gelmírez.

A second "golden age" of sculpture in Santiago de Compostela began in the 1160's with the accession of Pedro Gudestéiz as archbishop, the financial support of Ferdinand II, and the leadership of Master Matthew as head of the masons' shop. Generations of scholars have argued about the date when Matthew began work in Santiago and whether he was a native Galician or Leonese or a foreigner who came along the pilgrimage road. Since he was given a generous lifetime contract by Ferdinand II in 1168 and signed the lintel of the west portal in 1188, we know he spent that time in Santiago. After an examination of his style and the cathedral fabric, it may be argued that he had worked on the cathedral for some time before Ferdinand's donation. He could have been one of the men trained in the cathedral school and sent abroad for study, for his portal shows a familiarity with contemporary work all over western Europe. On the other hand, the features of the portal which can be related directly to French schools are items of composition or iconography which could have been suggested by the chapter or the archbishop. Master Matthew's technique, his style, and his vision of man are highly individual and do not indicate an apprenticeship in any of the northern schools. He is a southern artist.

In the *Pórtico de la Gloria* many diverse features are combined. The architecture is inspired by the Cistercian and proto-Gothic structures of France, and the ribbed vault is used on a large scale for the first time in Spain. In its purely architectural decorative features, a profound influence of Moorish architectural decoration, as seen in the work of the Almohades, is found. The individual figures in the sculpture, however, are both a development out of the pilgrimage style of the early twelfth-century Compostela and a three-dimensional version of the humanistic tendencies seen in manuscript illuminations beginning about 1160. Matthew has to some extent translated the painting into stone as the earlier masons did the ivories.

Master Matthew's portal on the Cathedral of Santiago is the masterpiece of twelfth-century sculpture in Spain and one of the great monuments of all western Europe. It consists of an undercroft, an open porch between two towers, and a gallery. The undercroft (used as a chapel and now called the *catedral vieja*) was necessary because of the sharp drop in ground level from east to west under the cathedral. It was connected to the church by an interior staircase on each side opening into the nave. A sharp change in sculpture style may be noted in the chapel and in the last bay of the nave and undoubtedly indicates Matthew's presence in the shop.

In the portico the four-part division of the cathedral façade was changed by Matthew into a three-part division. The lack of harmony in proportions occurred because the large center opening simply included the two original center doors; thus the side doors, each half the width of the center, seem cramped. The porch measures approximately fifty-seven feet by thirteen and one-half feet.

The central portal represents the Glory of Christ and the salvation of man through his sacrifice. The Apocalyptic vision with the four beasts and twenty-four elders is combined with the new vision of Christ showing his wounds, flanked by the angels of the Passion and the Elect crowned in Paradise, a theme created at Abbot Suger's church of St. Denis near Paris. On the north portal, figures are surrounded by foliage and are led to Paradise by angels; on the south, the Damned and Elect are separated by Christ and St. Michael and again the souls are led to Paradise. Four angels trumpet the Last Judgment, and others sing praises. Below are statue columns supporting the portal and leading into the church with prophets, kings, and apostles representing the Old and New Testaments, led by Moses and St. Peter. Santiago is seated on the central column welcoming, as it were, the pilgrims to his shrine. The entire portico rests on the backs of ferocious monsters. The architectural elements are enriched by spiral marble columns, a magnificent tree of Jesse in marble on the trumeau, rich foliage carving of mouldings, and a splendid set of capitals ornamented with foliage and fantastic beasts. Kneeling at the foot of the trumeau and facing the altar is a secular figure, traditionally called Master Matthew. On the lintel is the following inscription:

"In the year of the Incarnation of our Lord, 1188, Era 1226, April 1, the lintel of the principal portal of the Church of St. James was placed by Master Matthew who was master from the foundation of this portal."

This great portal could be seen from afar at the top of the stairs, for the cathedral was never closed in the Middle Ages. The exterior façade was destroyed in the sixteenth and eighteenth centuries, first when doors were placed in the portal, and then when the Baroque façade was added. Recent excavations have unearthed parts of the original decoration. On this façade, the archivolts of the portals corresponding to those of the interior were decorated with foliage, angels, and repeated Moorish horseshoe and keyhole arches. This decorative system spread through Galicia and may be seen in the parish churches of Compostela and at the cathedral of Orense.

Master Matthew combined Spanish and southern French Romanesque sculpture, Almohade decoration, Cistercian architecture, Sugerian iconography, and even elements from decorative arts into a personal style of great distinction. A towering genius, Matthew dominated not only the artists working for him, but also sculpture in Galicia for two hundred years. Some individual masons can be identified in this shop, and after Matthew's death they continued to turn out uninspired copies of his work.

Although many projects were under way at the end of the twelfth century, Matthew's shop went into an immediate decline when he was no longer in charge. His death or disability must have occurred shortly after 1188. Even in the tympanum of the *Pórtico de la Gloria,* a loss of quality is apparent, and such important sculpture would not have been entrusted to a lesser workman had the master been in full control. Even a great rush to finish the work for the funeral of Ferdinand II in 1188 is not enough to explain the uninspired ponderousness of the angels of the Passion, for example. Lesser masters had the responsibility for completing the choir stalls, cloister, and the gallery over the *Pórtico* at the turn of the century. Neither Master Matthew nor Archbishop Pedro Suárez saw the completion of their work or the final consecration of the cathedral in 1211.

The sculpture of the *Pórtico de la Gloria* retains its polychromy; and although none of the painting dates from the twelfth century, it serves as a reminder that the other arts also flourished in Santiago de Compostela. The *Pórtico de la Gloria* must have been repainted often, and contracts for painting it have survived from the fifteenth and the seventeenth centuries. The repaintings probably followed more or less the scheme of the original work. A few other references to painting may be found in twelfth-century records; for example, the chapel of the canons built by Gelmírez was beautifully painted according to the *Historia Compostelana.* A painter, as well as a glazier, is mentioned in a later list of the officials of the cathedral shop. Much as we in the twentieth century may prefer fine ashlar masonry and beautiful granite walls, we must remember that both decorative and didactic paintings covered the walls. An idea of the appearance of the twelfth-century building can be gained from the Pantheon of the Kings in the Church of San Isidoro in León.

Santiago de Compostela was famous in the twelfth century and later for work in precious materials, especially gold, silver, enamels, and jet; and we have already noted the early organization of these artists and craftsmen into guilds. Tantalizing references to precious objects abound in the *Historia Compostelana* and other sources, but not one of the pieces described has survived. The enamel altar of Santo Domingo de Silos, now in the Provincial Museum of Burgos, barely suggests the splendors of the high altar of the Cathedral of Santiago de Compostela. The many objects in jet from the fifteenth, sixteenth, and seventeenth centuries are a reminder of the importance of that Compostelan specialty. Jet itself was considered to have magical properties, especially in warding off the evil eye, and had been used as an amulet by the Romans. When it was "Christianized" in Galicia, the efficacy of the material combined with Christian symbols made it a potent charm, and it was widely sought after and distributed. Embroidery and the sewing of ecclesiastical vestments were other important crafts in Compostela. That Compostela was a center of book production in the twelfth century is apparent from surviving manuscripts such as the *Tumbo A* of the cathedral. The scribes and illuminators in the scriptoria of Compostela were the equals of any in Europe, and their work indicates the high level of education achieved under Gelmírez and continued by his successors.

The donations made by Gelmírez to the cathedral, probably in 1122, recorded in the *Historia Compostelana* indicate the kind of objects considered appropriate as offerings, most of which were probably produced in Santiago de Compostela.

───────────────

". . . Four citterns made in the Greek style; four pontifical copes; twelve other beautiful silk copes; two sets of pontifical vestments with all their accessories, three similar sets which were given away: one to Hugo, Bishop of Oporto, who had formerly been the archdeacon of the Church of Santiago, one to Nuño, Bishop of Mondoñedo, who had been the treasurer of the Church of the Apostle, and the third to Geraldo, Bishop of Salamanca, his suffragan. Also two dalmatics; a deacon's chasuble of black and one of purple; two Evangelaries with silver covers; one Evangelary whose gold cover was damaged and which the Archbishop restored; a silver missal; an Epistle and a wine pitcher of the same metal; a large golden belt; two silver coffers, one of which, it is said, contains the head of St. James Minor; another box of ivory; another of gilded metal admirably worked with glass incrustations; a precious coffer of gold which the Archbishop bought for three thousand sueldos and afterwards gave to Pope Calixtus; a relic of the True Cross encased in silver which Queen Urraca, daughter of King Alfonso VI, gave him, and he later gave to the Bishop of Turin; three chalices of silver and one of gold which, for the good of his church, he gave to the Pope; a censer of gold which he also gave for the good of his church; another golden censer he had made from his own personal money to replace the first one; three silver pitchers for use during the Mass; an antiphonary, a book of services and missal; three breviaries, a book of Lenten Offices, two benedictionals, the *Libre regulae Pastoralis,* the *Vita Episcoporum;* canons; a book of sentences; another of *Fide S. Trinitatis,* another book of sentences; and, finally, another book with the offices for the entire year." (*Historia Compostelana,* Book II, chapter 57)

———————————

This list of books had an added importance since it is our best indication of the contents of the cathedral library in Gelmírez' time.

That Santiago de Compostela was a center of learning in Spain in the twelfth century is not at all surprising considering its religious and political importance, economic strength, and patronage of the arts. The international character of the population and the constant influx of pilgrims created a stimulating environment which could not help being an educational experience for residents or visitors. Not only canonry and cloister but the entire city could be thought of as a great school.

At first Santiago de Compostela had two competing schools—the monastic school of St. Marín's and the cathedral grammar school—but soon the cathedral school gained the ascendancy, although, like Chartres, in spite of its important role in the twelfth century, it did not develop into a university. (The present University of Santiago de Compostela was a sixteenth-century foundation.) The cathedral school was primarily intended to train the clergy and apparently included only grammar and rhetoric. Diego Gelmírez was "instructed in letters in the church of Santiago and then educated in the household of the Bishop" (*Historia Compostelana,* Book II, chapter 2). When he became bishop, he required all canons to study if they lacked the education to perform their duties. He introduced oratory and logic into the curriculum and sent members of the clergy to France to study grammar and philosophy. The schoolmaster was one of the dignitaries of the chapter along with the dean, cantor, archdeacons, seven cardinals, and treasurer. Gerardo, or Giraldo, who wrote the *Historia Compostelana* beginning with Book I, chapter 83 (the period after 1113), was educated in France and was also schoolmaster. He was succeeded by Rainero of Pistoia who had studied in Winchester, England, and came to Compostela on a pilgrimage in 1134. Like so many others, Rainero was persuaded to remain in Compostela; however, he was so highly thought of at home that considerable tension arose between the archbishop of Compostela and the bishop of Pistoia. The remarkable and unique gift of a relic of St. James to the Cathedral of Pistoia in order to placate the bishop (one is tempted to say in exchange for Rainero) attests to the importance given to education and a great teacher in Compostela in the twelfth century. Rainero rose to become a cardinal of the cathedral. Among other notables in Compostela were Robert of Salerno, a physician who may have done some teaching for a brief period, and a Master Raucelinus. (No convincing evidence exists, however, that Raucelinus was the famous nominalist theologian Roscelin.)

More specific information on the state of education in Santiago de Compostela survives from the later twelfth century. In 1170 the duties of the schoolmaster were defined.

By then he had many more responsibilities than the educational program. He actually acted as chancellor of the chapter with the responsibility of the seal and thus of authenticating all official documents and even many private papers. His other duties included arranging the daily lessons for Matins. In supervising the education of clerics, choir boys, and the entire city and diocese, he was assisted by a preceptor. The preceptor did the actual teaching, consisting essentially of grammar, and edited the letters of the chapter, assisted the choir, and corrected their errors of pronunciation and accent. The schoolmaster had the same income from the cathedral as the other dignitaries of the chapter, while the preceptor's salary was sixty sueldos a year. Because of the enormous amount of work and responsibility, the schoolmaster was assigned not one but two prebends and was served by a *doblero* who was to substitute for him in the choir during daily services and on other occasions when duties were heavy.

Study abroad was encouraged throughout the twelfth century. Gelmírez kept abreast of developments in France and Italy by traveling to Rome, Cluny, and Paris; and he encouraged his clergy to study abroad to perfect their knowledge of theology. In the second half of the century, this study was regulated by the chapter. Rules were established in a meeting on July 30, 1169, and are preserved in *Tumbo B* of the cathedral archives:

"Inasmuch as it is necessary for the clergy to guard the majesty of the church, so must they zealously apply themselves to study, since it is fitting that the status of the church is best preserved by men of letters and philosophers who are shining examples of good character. As far as is possible the various hardships which stand in the way

144

of the students and liberals sons of the church shall be reduced, for there are several who, although they approach study with eager minds, yet oppressed as they are by the great burden of poverty, do not manage to achieve what they aspire to. Hence, invariably, good intentions come to naught when want, the inhibitor of liberality, denies them exercise. Therefore, we, canons of the Church of Compostela, in all devotion, deliberating on our position, have decreed that learning should be cultivated and have attempted without laying a burden on the community to provide for our brothers who wish to master the study of liberal arts.

"Therefore, having gained the generous and pious assent of our Holy Father the Archbishop Peter II, we have laid down and decreed by scriptural oath that it should be confirmed that the clerics of our chapter and the prebendaries of the church who aspire to literary studies, provided that they conscienciously remain, in their study of literature, within the limits laid down for them by the chapter wherever they are, are always to receive during their absence an equal share of the money from the offerings on the altar which is assigned by decree to the community with those remaining in the church, so that with their want in some measure overcome, they may apply themselves all the more eagerly to the cultivation of learning; and having been sent, so to speak, happily and fruitfully abroad, they may open their minds to the cultivation of virtue, now that they are free from financial worries. For thus our flourishing church will rejoice, like a mother, in her wise sons; and when worthy heirs succeed, her spiritual status will not be marred.

"And we decree that this should be observed only with respect to our prebendaries who are accustomed to bear the daily burdens and to live with us, provided that neither the church nor we shall suffer loss or harm, which everyone should avoid, when the barriers are removed by this far-seeing and praiseworthy decision. For anyone else who, either through his own powerful influence, or because of his high birth, or through the intervention of some other powerful person, or through any sort of flattery, challenging this dispensation, attempts to destroy such a proper and necessary institution, so that like one of our prebendaries, he may strive, with as much rashness as impudence, to gain for himself the aforesaid favor, granted out of charity and honor, let him know that he is not one of our order, and he is deprived entirely of assistance from our church. And let him know, moreover, that he is excommunicated on the authority of the excellent Archbishop Peter. Moreover, if anyone— may it not happen to us—through an inclination to take more freedom, puts forward an imaginary program of study, as soon as they are known to be acting dishonorably, in their absence the chapter shall order them by letter to be recalled from their pretended study. And if they refuse to return at the first call, then straightway we judge them to be deprived of their benefice until we learn from a reliable report that they are leading an honorable life and pursuing an earnest intent to study." (López Ferreiro, Vol. IV, app. 40)

A vital part of the educational program, based as it was on analysis of the writing of the past, was the possession of a library. Books were expensive, difficult, and time-consuming to produce. In contrast to the great Roman libraries such as Alexandria's or the enormous Moorish collections such as those found in Córdoba, the Christians had only small monastic or cathedral libraries, numbering at best a few hundred volumes. The cathedral library at Santiago de Compostela in the early twelfth century probably held about two hundred books. The twenty books listed in the *Historia Com-postelana* as donations of Gelmírez included Gospels, missals, brevaries, and two collections of "sentences." These books of "sentences" are of special interest because they indicate that Gelmírez was acquiring for the cathedral library the most modern tools of scholarship. The sentences were a revolutionary new technique in scholarship introduced in the late eleventh century by Anselm of Laon and continued in the twelfth century in Paris. This work culminated in the *Sentences* of Peter Lombard and the *Sic et Non* of Abelard. The sentences were the first attempt systematically to arrange and analyze the commentaries on church doctrine and scripture which had been accumulated over the centuries. These codifications provided the basis for the development of scholastic philosophy by the next generation.

Literary activity in Compostela during the twelfth century was as significant as the work in sculpture and architecture. The cathedral school encouraged the production of prose works, including sermons or homilies and lives of the saints common in the Middle Ages. Letters were written with great care, as witnessed by the schoolmaster's duty to edit them, and must also be included among the prose literature of the time. (Pope Calixtus' ringing call to crusade is an example of the style.) The prologues of many documents, such as the statement on the benefits of education in the 1169 decree, are fine essays showing considerable literary skill.

The major prose work surviving from the early twelfth century in Compostela is the *Historia Compostelana,* the life and acts of Diego Gelmírez, first archbishop, covering the period up to about 1139. The *Historia Compostelana* is not only an admirable example of historical writing and an apology for the great churchman, but it shows a narrative style of grace and vigor. Gelmírez' confidants, Nuño and Hugo, began it at his request and worked on it until 1112 when they became bishops of Mondoñedo and Oporto, respectively. Giraldo, whom we have already seen as the canon responsible for the educational program of the chapter, continued the book. The *Historia Compostelana* is not, as are most records of the period, a terse account of works and days, but rather it is an exciting narrative, full of drama and vivid reporting of events and conversations. The story of the rebellion of 1117, for example, is told by Giraldo in a brisk narrative style worthy of a good reporter. Editorial comment on the virtues of the archbishop and the evils of the populace does not intrude too heavily on the narrative.

Drama, too, was beginning in Santiago de Compostela, springing from the natural desire to animate or reinforce passages of the scripture or the liturgy. The festivals and processions of the cathedral were to some extent a drama; and the ritual of the choir itself with the large numbers of clerics taking part was like a great pageant, a kind of liturgical ballet. The sculpture of the *Pórtico de la Gloria* seems to reflect a theatrical instinct on the part of the church, for the figures seem to come alive, to move, to react to one another, to turn, even to smile. They may even reflect actual performances. The first recorded dramatic performance in Compostela dates from the sixteenth century. In 1512, payments were made for dramas performed during Lent and Epiphany, especially the Arrival of the Three Magi. The three Magi were given a place of importance in Compostela because they were considered to have been the first pilgrims in Christianity.

Poetry rather than prose had always been the popular literary form in Galicia. Poetry in Santiago de Compostela has been the subject of study partly because of its important role in the development of Portugese literature and the Gallego-Portugese language. Native songs also existed in the sixth century when the singing of songs with magical and diabolical meanings was prohibited in the Galician churches. As early as the ninth century Galician words appear in Latin documents; however, Galician as a written language really did not come into being until the late twelfth and early thirteenth centuries. When Castilian began to replace Latin as the official language for use in documents, history, and epic literature, Galician was still used for poetry. Not until Ferdinand and Isabel made Castilian the official language at the end of the fifteenth century did Galician decline in importance as a literary language in the Iberian peninsula.

Three themes run through Galician poetry: satire, friendship, and love. The cynical, racy satirical poems reflect the popular art of the day. The songs of friendship are an original Galician contribution to troubadour literature, and their typically Galician spirit is revealed by the poets' interest in nature and the open air. The indigenous Celtic poetry never completely died out in northwestern Spain and also influenced Galician lyrics. These lyrics had an undisciplined verse form, relying on a repetition of phrases for their slow-moving rhythm. The poems are remarkable for their concreteness, with many references to specific objects, places, or events, and for the mood of sadness, even of nostalgia which permeates them. Life is varied, contradictory, and violent; the conflict between the mystics' negation of the world and a human joy in life seems irreconcilable. This mood of wistful sadness was also characteristic of Moorish secular poetry which flourished in the eleventh century.

Galician poets also knew the aristocratic love songs of Provençal poetry. Not only troubadors and *jongleurs* but people like William of Aquitaine, the "prince of troubadors," made the pilgrimage to Santiago de Compostela. (William died in the nave of the cathedral during Mass.) Raymond and Henry of Burgundy must also have had poets in their retinues. From Provence, the Galician troubador learned the cult of courtly love and chivalry and an awareness of subtler emotions; and he learned to use a more formal, even artificial, literary structure. Even so, the Galician love songs are less personal and less erotic than the Provençal songs and also differ in having a popular character and sense of melancholy and mystery.

The earliest preserved songs date from the second half of the twelfth century, and large numbers of poems have survived from the later Middle Ages. Some individual authors are known, the greatest of whom was Aryas Núñez, a cleric and resident of Compostela in the time of Archbishop Pedro Suárez. His intricate poetry is characterized by its spontaneous beauty and grace. Eighteen of his songs are included in the *Vatican Canionero.* Other poets are Bernal de Bonaval, Sancho I of Portugal, the son of Alfonso VII, Xohan Airas, Pedro da Ponte, Roi Paes de Ribela, and Pedro de Ver. In these Gallego-Portugese *cancioneros* of the thirteenth and fourteenth centuries, themes of courtly love, friendship, satire, and mockery are treated in a rich and varied language.

Naturally, important poetry was composed in Latin as well as in the vernacular. Religious poetry, as is to be expected, reached a high level. The beautiful hymn, *Salve Regina,* one of the masterpieces of Christian religious poetry, was composed by Bishop Pedro Mezonzo (died in 1003). Poetry of all nations must have been heard in Compostela in the hymns of the pilgrims. The earliest recorded pilgrims' hymn is found in the Calixtine Codex. The author of *Dum*

Pater familias (f. 193 r.) makes an elaborate play on the name of James in all six Latin cases.

When Alfonso the Wise began *Las Cántigas,* or *Hymns to the Virgin Mary,* it was the Galician not the Castilian language which he chose to use. At first the hymns seem a "spontaneous outburst of simple praise"; however, all possible refinements of writing were employed to achieve effects of simplicity and expressiveness. Actually, Alfonso did not compose all of the *Cántigas.* The collection of 420 songs was begun in 1257, and several poets contributed to it.

Music is, of course, intimately connected with lyric poetry and hymns. Compostela was in the twelfth century one of the leading centers of music in the Western world. This musical supremacy is attested to both by the preservation of manuscripts containing music in the cathedral archives and by the most detailed representation of musical instruments in the twelfth century in sculpture. The *Codex Calixtinus* reflects the musical life of the city. It contains offices, masses, and processions dedicated to St. James, and also has the earliest music for more than one voice in Spain, if not in Europe. The clergy of Santiago de Compostela readily accepted the Roman rite and developed a liturgy with a remarkable local quality, even incorporating Galician melodies into the music. The *Codex Calixtinus* preserves four processionals from the Office of St. James known as *conducta Sancti Jacobi.* Three of them may have been composed in Santiago. Of great interest is the polyphonic music for solemn procession with voices accompanied by instrumental music. Whereas the offices are almost pure Gregorian, the *conducti* were based on dance melodies. Dances such as those still performed in the cathedral of Seville may have been interjected into the ceremony. In the same Codex is a trope, *Congaudiant catholici,* on the *Benedicamus Domino* which may be the oldest three-part composition in existence; it has been ascribed, however, to Master Albertus, a Parisian. The richest source for the study of Galician religious music as well as poetry are the four surviving manuscripts of the *Cantigas,* three of which contain musical notation. The music as well as the poetry is derived from many sources, the most common being the Western *virelai* and the Moorish *zajal.*

Compostelan music may be appreciated by studying the elders of the *Pórtico de la Gloria.* They represent a heavenly orchestra and choir, undoubtedly reflecting what the artist saw and heard in the cathedral when the seventy-two canons, all the abbots and priors of the diocese, and the "clerics of the choir," making an assembly of hundreds, celebrated the Mass on the great festivals of the church.

The poems of the troubadours, too, were most certainly meant to be sung and perhaps even to be given an instrumental introduction or accompaniment. Of the *Siete canciones de amor* attributed to Martin Codax, six survive with music. Although the songs are thirteenth century, the melodies resemble Mozarabic penitential songs and may, therefore, be regarded as examples of native Spanish music. These Galician songs are among the earliest known examples of secular music.

Instrumental groups of some complexity were assembled by the end of the twelfth century, and Compostela became a center of instrumental composition and performance. It will be recalled that the first of Gelmírez's gifts to the cathedral were four citherns in the "Greek style" (perhaps lyres). The archbishop's palace contains a rare illustration in sculpture of the place of music in secular and ecclesiastical courts in the early thirteenth century. Scenes on the sculptured corbels of the hall show guests at dinner enjoying musical entertainment. The selection and arrangement of instruments lack the sophistication seen in the sculpture of the elders of the *Pórtico de la Gloria;* however, included in the ensemble are an organistrum, guitar, cithern, harp, aulos, and eight violas.

The study of the development of the musical instruments themselves is exceptionally difficult since few actual instruments have survived, thus forcing the historian to depend for information on representations in sculpture and painting. One of the most important of these sources is the *Pórtico de la Gloria,* for many of the instruments used during the twelfth century are held by the twenty-four elders. The detail, the variety, and the care with which the instruments are carved suggests either that the artist had considerable interest in music or that the clerical patron was particularly devoted to the art. Master Matthew carved these figures himself, another indication of the importance which either Matthew or his patron attached to these heavenly musicians. The selection of instruments represented on the *Pórtico de la Gloria* is particularly interesting. Stringed instruments were preferred in the Middle Ages, since the harp had been played by David and, therefore, gained added sanctity through its biblical associations. On the *Pórtico* even the violas are not played with bows but by plucking in imitation of the harp. The delicate pizzicato of the harps, citherns, and violas would contrast with the low drone of the organistrum. Four magnificent trumpets are also represented in the hands of the angels who announce the Day of Wrath. Percussion instruments, especially bells, tambourines, and castanets, were introduced by the Moors. That they were in general use in Europe in the twelfth century is indicated by the representations of them in other sculpture. They are not, however, found in Master Matthew's orchestra.

153

Even the most superficial study leads one to the realization that Santiago de Compostela was a great center of the arts in western Europe; and because of its unique relationship with Islam, it also provided a bridge between East and West. Under such conditions the richest imaginable cultural life could thrive. Although centered in the episcopal court and in the church, the great festivals of St. James affected citizens in every walk of life. The splendid flowering of Christian culture in the twelfth century was dependent on peace and prosperity, a cliché which is given more emphasis by the contrast of the ages of Gelmírez and Suárez with the periods which succeeded them. The greatness of the city's development was also dependent on a free exchange of people and ideas, enhanced by the ferment and the tolerant attitude toward foreigners caused by the pilgrimage.

VII.

Postscript:
Santiago de Compostela through the Centuries

The history of Santiago de Compostela after the heroic age of the pilgrimages in the eleventh and twelfth centuries has few glorious chapters. Pedro Suárez died in 1206, and the cathedral was completed and finally consecrated in 1211 by Archbishop Pedro Muñiz. Shortly thereafter, two important religious orders were established in Santiago de Compostela by their founders. In 1214, St. Francis of Assisi visited the shrine of St. James and founded the first Franciscan monastery in Spain. In the 1220's, St. Dominic also came to the city as a pilgrim and established the Dominican order. The convent of Santa Clara was founded in 1260. Compostela was visited by many distinguished pilgrims in the thirteenth century. Noble and royal pilgrims included St. Louis of France (Joinville wrote that the king had as much devotion to St. James as to Sainte Genevieve) and his mother, Blanche of Castile, the kings of Portugal, and Count Raymond of Toulouse. King Edward I of England also made the pilgrimage and was knighted in Burgos by Alfonso the Wise. The struggle between Compostela and Córdoba finally ended in 1236 when St. Ferdinand captured Córdoba and returned the bells of the cathedral, which had been carried off by Almanzor, on the shoulders of Moorish captives. Juan

155

Arias who governed the see between 1237 and 1266 was an able administrator, and both the city and the see prospered under his rule; however, his death was followed by a period of anarchy in the city, which became more serious as civil war spread throughout the kingdom in the second half of the century.

Compostela did not escape the religious and political crises of the fourteenth century. The century began auspiciously when the archbishop of Santiago called and presided over the Council of Salamanca where the Feast of the Immaculate Conception was established and the University of Salamanca was organized. This was a minor interlude, however, for the church was torn by the "Babylonian Captivity" of the papacy and then the Great Schism. The claims of rival popes were particularly unsettling in Galicia; in fact, the economic and political consequences were calamitous. Over the years many donations of property—fields, churches, and monasteries—had been made to the cathedrals; thus by the fourteenth century bishops administered and depended for revenue on lands lying within each others' sees. Furthermore, in Galicia some bishoprics were administered by the bishops of Portugal, and some Portuguese bishoprics belonged to Santiago de Compostela. At the time of the Schism, Urban VI was supported by Portugal, England, Italy, Austria, Bohemia, and Hungary; Clement VII, by Castile, Aragón, France, Scotland, and Sicily. The archbishop of Santiago de Compostela supported Clement and voted for him in the Council of 1381. Thus the Portuguese clergy ruled by Santiago felt justified in calling the Compostelan archbishop schismatic and defying him, while the bishops of Galicia who were under Braga denounced their Portuguese archbishop as schismatic. Ecclesiastical government practically collapsed.

As if this state of affairs were not bad enough, the political situation in Spain had also fallen into anarchy. The great crusading days of St. Ferdinand in the first half of the thirteenth century and of Alfonso XI, from 1310 to 1350, ended with Alfonso's death. Pedro the Cruel moved the court to Seville and turned over the government of Galicia to his supporter Fernando de Castro; however, Pedro hated the de Castro family and soon began to mistrust Fernando. He had de Castro murdered and appropriated his castles and troops. Then Pedro perpetrated one of his most sensational crimes in Compostela: he had Archbishop Suero Gómez and the dean of the Chapter, Pedro Álvarez, murdered in 1366 because he suspected them of supporting D. Enrique de Trastámara. All the churches of the city were closed in mourning over this atrocity, and the people heard Mass in the Church of Santa María del Conjo (the twelfth-century church built in the suburbs by Gelmírez); thus the expression "to hear Mass in Conjo" to express calm hopelessness entered the language, recalling this sacrilegious murder. When Pedro was assassinated in 1369, Archbishop Rodrigo de Moscoso recognized Enrique, count of Trastámara, as king. The citizens of Compostela, however, had supported the de Castros and opposed Archbishop Moscoso (whom they had on occasion driven from the city); and they were backed by the king of Portugal. The rebellion was put down by Enrique de Trastámara with great severity. Later in the chaotic fourteenth century the duke of Lancaster, who had married a Spanish princess, claimed Castile through his wife; and in 1386 he invaded Galicia and occupied Compostela. After the Trastámaras finally regained control, Compostela was restored to royal favor.

In spite of the civil wars the pilgrimage to Santiago de Compostela continued. St. Isabel of Portugal and St. Bridget of Sweden, members of the French royal family, and the duke of Burgundy all came as pilgrims; Charles V founded the Chapel of the King of France in the cathedral with a huge donation at the time of his death in 1380; and in Paris the Queen Jeanne d'Evreux founded a hospital for pilgrims returning from Compostela.

The fifteenth century saw the widespread distress among the citizens of Santiago continued; the city consistently supported the losing side in dynastic struggles and rebelled against the archbishops. Neither of the first two Fonseca archbishops was able to control the see, and the city survived sieges so fierce that a catapult was even mounted on the roof of the cathedral. The oppression of citizens became intolerable; and a "Holy Brotherhood," which included members of the cathedral chapter, was formed to fight the nobility and destroy their castles. When Isabel was finally proclaimed queen in 1474, she was supported by the archbishop (the second Alonso Fonseca), but he had not even been able to enter Santiago for ten years. Galicia and Portugal had supported the claims of Isabel's half-sister, Juana; nevertheless, the royal family made pilgrimages to the shrine of St. James and built a splendid hospital for pilgrims in Compostela.

In spite of political difficulties, the economic and cultural life of the city revived during the fifteenth century. Many new streets and squares with fountains were laid out; and shops, houses, hospitals, and hostels were rebuilt. The cathedral was repaired and reroofed and the interior refurbished. The guilds flourished, and many of their records survive. A Holy Year in 1434, with a safe conduct for pilgrims proclaimed by Juan II, inspired renewed fervor and commercial activity. Among the famous pilgrims of the fifteenth century were San Bernardino of Siena and St. Anthony. St.

Vincent Ferrer was also devoted to St. James and lived in the monastery of Santo Domingo in 1412.

One of the greatest Spanish humanists and patrons of the arts, Alonso García de Santa María, was the dean of Santiago during the early years of the century. The dean was a converted Jew who later became bishop of Burgos. He attended the Council of Basle in 1434 and was responsible for bringing the architect Hans of Cologne (Juan de Colonia) to Burgos. Thus, he should have credit for establishing one of the most important artistic dynasties in Spain and for introducing the German late Gothic style into Castile.

During the sixteenth century, in spite of royal indifference and injustice, the arts flourished in Compostela under the patronage of archbishop Alonso IV (the third Fonseca, 1509–24). The cathedral was remodeled with the addition of towers, the Chapels of the Immaculate Conception, the Holy Cross, and the Holy Sacrament, the western doorway in front of the *Pórtico de la Gloria,* a new cloister by Rodrigo Gil de Hontañón, and superb bronze grills and screens for the choir. A Jesuit monastery and college and the hospital of San Roque were also built. The hospital founded by Ferdinand and Isabel was completed, and the archbishop's palace was enlarged. Educational institutions such as the College of San Jeronimo (1510), the College of Fonseca (1540), and the university (1532) were founded, and splendid buildings built to house them. Less spectacular—but equally tangible—evidence of intellectual activity was the new edition of the missal and breviary published in Compostela. The international humanistic tone of Fonseca's court is indicated by the fact that the archbishop was one of the patrons of Erasmus.

The Renaissance was short lived in Compostela, however, for the country was swept by the bubonic plague in 1560; and plagues, famine, and military disasters continued for the rest of the century. Galicia suffered from the wars with England at the end of the century more than the rest of Spain because it was vulnerable to the English sea power. By 1585, Sir Francis Drake was harassing the coast. In 1588, La Coruña was the supply base and then a haven for the wreckage of the great Armada. The Armada's defeat by storms and the British navy was followed by an invasion of fourteen thousand English troops led by Drake. Their goal was the destruction of Santiago de Compostela, which the English called "the principal emporium of Papal superstitions." The relics of St. James were removed from their ancient tomb and reburied behind the altar by Archbishop Juan de San-clemente and a false story was circulated that they had been taken to Orense. Compostela did not fall to the English; but in the forty years of chaos that followed the attack, the hiding place of the relics was forgotten.

Plague, starvation, Turkish raids on the coasts, more English raids, the destruction of the Galician navy, and war with France filled the first half of the seventeenth century. Nevertheless, under the energetic leadership of Archbishop Maximilian of Austria (1602–14) work continued on the cathedral. A new choir was carved by Juan Dávila to replace the Romanesque stone choir, fragments of which were re-used in the *Puerta Santa* of 1611; the inner stairs of the western façade of the cathedral were built, and the bell tower, cupola, and clock tower were finished. In the city, the College of San Clemente was founded.

During the second half of the century Compostela grew and flourished again. Fortunately for the economic life of the city, the *Voto de Santiago* was re-established by Philip IV. The pilgrimage, on the other hand, was made very difficult for anyone traveling from or through France, because the French kings issued edicts in 1617 and 1687 prohibiting pilgrimages to Santiago. The Spanish kings followed a course of political folly leading to economic ruin; nevertheless, magnificent architectural projects were undertaken and completed in Compostela. The city assumed much of its present appearance. Religious establishments dominated the cityscape; their severe granite walls were broken with sculpture which had all the massive exuberance of a provincial Baroque style. The old monastic foundations of St. Francis and San Martin Pinario were rebuilt; and the church of St. Martin, the Augustinian monastery, and the Mercedarian convent were erected. The architect Canon José de Vega y Verdugo designed the Plaza de la Quintana, the portals and the east façade of the cathedral. Within the cathedral the new high altar with its silver frontal attests to the high level of skill maintained through the centuries by Compostelan craftsmen.

The building activity continued through the first half of the eighteenth century. The splendid Churrigueresque façade of the cathedral was begun by Fernando de Casas y Nóvoa in 1738 and finished in 1750. The convent of Santa Clara, the monasteries of Santo Domingo and San Pelayo were rebuilt, and the Carmelite convent and the Chapel of All Souls were constructed. Twelfth-century churches were restored, and ancient streets such as the Rua Villar were lined with houses and arcades. New buildings were erected for the university in 1750 and the chapter in 1758. The *Sala Capitular,* the Chapel of the Virgin of the Pillar, the north transept portal, and the Communion Chapel were all added to the cathedral. The monumental heart of the city as it now appears was nearly completed with the construction of the city hall and seminary on the site of the old castle and prison in a section of the city walls opposite the cathedral. The high quality of eighteenth-century sculpture and decoration may be appreciated in the high altar and choir of St. Martin's or in the organs and altars of the cathedral.

Politically in the eighteenth and nineteenth centuries the Galicians still seemed determined to support the losing side. For example, James Stuart lived for a time in the Monastery of San Martin Pinario; and his presence gave the English an excuse to invade Galicia in 1719. They landed at Vigo, and Compostela was saved only by the mutiny of the Scottish troops. Throughout the century Spain continued to be embroiled in wars with France and England. During the Napoleonic Wars, Compostela fell to Marshal Soult in 1809. Although the city was soon liberated, the churches and libraries were pillaged and burned by the withdrawing French troops. Little other than the durable granite buildings survived the wanton destruction. The economic life of the city as well as of the church was dealt a severe blow by the abolition again of the *Voto de Santiago;* and the Exclaustration Act of 1835, which closed all the convents and monasteries, provided the coup de grace. Not only did many fine buildings fall into decay, but the remaining monastic libraries were scattered and destroyed.

The rediscovery of the relics of St. James, recognized as authentic by Pope Leo XIII in 1884, seemed to mark a turning point in the fortunes of Santiago de Compostela, for the city has fared well in the twentieth century. It escaped severe damage during the Civil War. The neglect of the nineteenth century suddenly became an advantage in the mid-twentieth century when the entire heart of the city was declared to be a national monument, a living museum. Under enlightened and scholarly archbishops and secular authorities Santiago de Compostela again plays a leading role in the cultural life of the nation, although the pilgrimages are more often inspired by historical or artistic interest in the city and its monuments than by a religious fervor.

Here, then, in the northwestern corner of the Iberian peninsula, apparently geographically isolated from the world, a city grew and flourished in the Romanesque period which even the cultured Moors respected. As the goal of thousands of pilgrims, it was an important focal point for the development of medieval culture. In the city, men from all nations could rub shoulders and exchange ideas. Some of the art and learning of the Moors, and with it the classical and Byzantine heritage, could be also imparted to the Western Christians while they were in Spain. Moorish art, architecture, engineering, science, mathematics, literature, music, and love of a better physical life spread back across the Pyrenees. Very western, however, was the demand for civil liberty and the rise of a middle class which we have seen in Santiago de Compostela.

As a city, Compostela in the twelfth century held a position it would never regain. It was a leader in architecture, literature, and music, and also in the economic, religious, and political life of the peninsula. It was the shrine of the patron of the Spanish people, a unifying force in a land divided into many kingdoms, a leader in the struggle for civil rights and political liberty, and a profound educational force. The combination of an enlightened archbishop, a wealthy clerical and secular population, and a relatively high level of education produced a city environment as stimulating as only a great metropolitan center can be. Santiago de Compostela, for a while, took a place among the centers of civilization.

Bibliography

Contemporary Sources

Liber Sancti Jacobi, Codex Calixtinus

David, Pierre. *Études sur le livre de Saint-Jacques.* Lisbon, 1946–49.

Moralejo, A., C. Torres Rodríguez, and J. Feo García. *Liber Sancti Jacobi, Codex Calixtinus.* Santiago de Compostela, 1951. Translation into Castilian with notes by A. Moralejo.

Vielliard, Jeanne. *Le guide du pèlerin de Saint-Jacques de Compostelle.* Macon, 1938. Latin text with French translation of Book V of the *Codex Calixtinus,* after manuscripts in Compostela and Ripoll (Archives of the Kingdom of Aragón in Barcelona).

Whitehill, Walter Muir. *Codex Calixtinus.* Santiago de Compostela, 1932–40. Transcription of the Latin text in the cathedral archives, with essays and notes by Whitehill, Jesús Carro García, and Germán Prado.

Historia Compostelana

Flórez, Enrique. *España Sagrada,* Vol. XX. Madrid, 1765. Transcription of the Latin text. (Index to *España Sagrada* by Angel González Palencia, Madrid, 1918.)

Suárez Lorenzo, Manuel, and José Campelo. *Historia Compostelana, Hechos de don Diego Gelmírez, primer arzo-*

bispo de Santiago. Santiago de Compostela, 1950. Translation into Castilian by Manuel Suárez, notes and introduction by José Campelo.

López Ferreiro, Antonio. *Historia de la Santa A. M. Iglesia de Santiago de Compostela.* Santiago de Compostela, 1898–1909. Each of the eleven volumes contains transcriptions of pertinent documents from the cathedral archives.

González Davila, Gil. *Teatro de las iglesias metropolitanas, y catedrales de los Reynos de las dos Castillas. Vidas de sus arzobispos, y obispos, y cosas memorables de sus sedes,* Vol. I. Santiago de Compostela, Madrid, 1645. Of antiquarian interest, a history of the see and a description of the cathedral and its furnishings.

Riobóo y Seixas (Villar de Francos), Antonio. *Analysis histórica cronológica de la primitiva erección, progresos y diversas re-edificaciones de la Santa Iglesia de Santiago.* Madrid, 1747.

Modern Studies

Alcolea, Santiago. *La catedral de Santiago de Compostela, los monumentos cardinales de España.* Madrid, 1948.

Altamira y Crevea, Rafael. *Historia de España y de la civilización española,* Vols. I and II. Barcelona, 1900–30.

Azcárate, José María de. "La Portada de las Platerías y el programa iconográfico de la catedral de Santiago," *Archivo español de arte,* Vol. XXXVI (1963), 1–20.

Biggs, Anselm Gordon. *Diego Gelmírez, First Archbishop of Compostela.* Catholic University of America *Studies in Medieval History,* new series, Vol. XII. Washington, D.C., 1949.

Caamaño Martínez, Jesús. *Contribución al estudio del Gótico en Galicia.* Valladolid, 1962.

Carreras y Candí, Francisco, ed. *Geografía general del Reino de Galicia.* Barcelona, 1932.

Castro y Quesada, Américo. *España en su historia; cristianos, moros, y judíos.* Buenos Aires, 1948. (*The Structure of Spanish History,* trans. by E. King [Princeton, 1954].)

———. *Santiago de España.* Buenos Aires, 1958.

Conant, Kenneth John. *The Early Architectural History of the Cathedral of Santiago de Compostela.* Cambridge, Harvard University Press, 1926.

Contreras y López de Ayala, Juan de, Marqués de Lozoya. *Historia del arte hispánico.* Barcelona, 1931.

Cossío, Manuel. *El Arte románico, siglos XI y XII; Summa Artis: Historia general del arte.* José Pijoan, ed. Madrid, 1944.

Del Campo, Luis. "La Medicina en el Camino de Santiago," *Príncipe de Viana,* 169–80.

Del Castillo López, Angel. *El Pórtico de la Gloria, estudio preliminar, Bibliofilos Gallegos, Colección Obradoiro,* Vol. I. Santiago de Compostela, 1949.

Del Río, Angel. *Historia de la literatura española.* 2 Vols. New York, 1960.

Estudios Jacobeos, Papers of the *Congreso Internacional de, Compostellanum,* Vol. X, No. 4 (extra number). Santiago de Compostela, 1965.

Fernández Sánchez, José M., and Francisco Freiro Barreiro. *Guia de Santiago y sus alrededores.* Santiago, 1885.

Filgueira Valverde, José. "Datos y conjeturas para la biografía del Maestro Mateo," *Guardernos de estudios gallegos,* Vol. III (1948), 49–69.

Ford, Jeremiah D. M. *Old Spanish Readings.* New York, 1911; reprint (Kraus), 1966.

Gaillard, Georges. *Les dèbuts de la sculpture romane es-*

pagnole, León-Jaca-Compostela. Paris, 1938.

Gill Farrés, Octavio. *Historia de la moneda española.* Madrid, 1959.

Gómez-Moreno, Manuel. *El arte románico española.* Madrid, 1934.

González López, Emilio. *Historia de la civilización española.* New York, 1959.

———. *Historia de la literatura española.* New York, 1962.

González Palencia, Angel. *Historia de la literatura arábigo-española.* Barcelona, 1928.

———. *Moros y cristianos en España medieval.* Madrid, 1945.

Granjel, Luis. *Historia de la medicina española.* Barcelona, 1962; Salamanca, 1969.

Gudiol Ricart, José, and Juan Antonio Gaya Nuño. *Arquitectura y escultura románicas, Ars Hispaniae,* Vol. V. Madrid, 1948.

Guerrero Lovillo, José. *Las Cántigas. Estudio arqueológico de sus miniaturas.* Madrid, 1949.

Heath, Sidney. *In the Steps of the Pilgrims.* New York, 1951 (originally *Pilgrim Life in the Middle Ages*).

Hell, Vera, and Helmut Hell. *The Great Pilgrimage of the Middle Ages, the Road to St. James.* New York, 1966.

Huidobro y Serna, Luciano. *Las Peregrinaciones Jacobeas.* 3 Vols. Madrid. 1950.

Iglesias Vilarelle, Antonio. "Los músicos del Pórtico de la Gloria." *El museo de Pontevedra,* Vol. VII (Pontevedra, 1952), 34–51.

Kendrick, Thomas. *St. James in Spain.* London, 1960.

King, Georgiana Goddard. *The Way of St. James.* New York, 1920.

Knowlton, John. "The Romanesque Sculpture of the Platerias Portal of the Cathedral of Santiago de Compostela." New York University, Institute of Fine Arts, thesis, 1939.

168

Lambert, Elie. "La peregrinación a Compostela y la arquitectura románica," *Archivo español de arte,* Vol. XVI (1943), 273–309.

———. *Le pèlerinage de Compostelle, Études d'histoire medieval.* Toulouse, 1958; Paris, 1959.

Lampérez y Romea, Vicent. *El antiguo palacio episcopal de Compostela.* Madrid, 1913.

Layton, Thomas A. *The Way of St. James.* London, 1976.

López Aydillo, Eugenio. *Presencia de Galicia en la historia de España.* Madrid, 1950.

López Ferreiro, Antonio. *El Pórtico de la Gloria.* Santiago de Compostela, 1893.

Mateo y Llopis, F. "Diplomática en Orense," *Cuadernos de estudios gallegos,* Vol. IX (1954), 319–40.

Mayer, Ernst. *Historia de las instituciones sociales y políticas de España y Portugal, durante los siglos V a XIV.* Madrid, 1925–26.

Mellini, Gian Lorenzo. *Maestro Mateo a Santiago de Compostela.* Florence, 1965.

Menéndez Pidal, Ramón. *Poema del Cid y otras gestas heroicas.* Madrid, 1923.

———. *Poema del Cid y otros monumentos de la primitiva poesía española.* Madrid, 1919.

———. *La España del Cid.* Madrid, 1929; revised edition in one volume, 1967. (*The Cid and his Spain,* trans. by H. Sunderland [London, 1934].)

———, ed. *Historia de España,* Vol. IV (E. Lévi-Provençal), Vol. V (E. Lévi-Provençal and L. Torres Balbás), Vol. VI (J. Pérez de Urbel and R. del Arco y Garay). Madrid, 1935–64.

———. *Poesía juglaresca y orígenes de las literaturas románicas* (6th ed. of *Poesía juglaresca y juglares*). Madrid, 1957.

Moreno Astray, Felix. *Santiago pintoresco.* Santiago, 1863.

————. *El viajero en la ciudad de Santiago.* Santiago de Compostela, 1865.

Mouriño, J., Marqués de Saluz. *La literatura medioeval en Galicia. Biblioteca de Estudios Gallegos,* Vol. III. Madrid, 1929.

Mullins, Edwin B. *The Pilgrimage to Santiago.* London, 1974.

Murguía, Manuel. *España, sus monumentos y artes—su naturaleza é historia, Galicia.* Barcelona, 1888.

Nesgaard, Ole. *Saint-Jacques de Compostelle et les dèbuts de la grande sculpture vers 1100.* Aarhus, 1962.

Otero Pedrayo, Ramón. *Historia de la cultura gallega.* Buenos Aires, 1939.

Pallarez Méndez, María del Carmen, and Ermelindo Portela Selva. *El bajo valle del Miño en los siglos XII y XIII, economía, agraria y estructura social.* Santiago de Compostela, 1971.

Porter, Arthur Kingsley. *Romanesque Sculpture of the Pilgrimage Roads.* Boston, 1923.

————. *Spanish Romanesque Sculpture.* New York, 1928.

Rodrigues Lapa, Manuel. *Das origens da poesía lirica em Portugal na idade média.* Lisbon, 1929.

————. *Escolania de Poesía Gallega,* Vol. I (1198–1346). Vigo, 1952.

Sánchez-Albornoz, Claudio. "La primitiva organización monetaria de León y Castilla," *Annuario, Historia de la derecho español,* Vol. V (1928), 313ff.

Sánchez Cantón, Francisco Javier. "La vida en Galicia en los tiempos del arte románico," *Cuadernos de estudios gallegos,* Vol. XVII (1962), 182–201.

Secret, Jean. *Saint-Jacques et les chemins de Compostelle.* Paris, 1955.

Silva, Rafael, and José R. Barreiro Fernández. *El Pórtico de la Gloria.* Santiago de Compostela, 1965.

Smith, Robert. *Medieval Agrarian Society in its Prime: Spain, The Cambridge Economic History of Europe* (eds. J. H. Clapham and E. Power), Vol. I. Cambridge, 1942.

Soldevila Zubiburu, Fernando. *Historia de España,* Vol. I. Barcelona, 1952–59.

Starkie, Walter. *The Road to Santiago; Pilgrims of St. James.* London, 1957; 2d ed., Los Angeles, 1965.

Stokstad, Marilyn. "El Pórtico de la Gloria of the Cathedral of Santiago de Compostela," University of Michigan, Ann Arbor, Michigan, dissertation, 1957.

Subirá, José. *Historia de la música.* Barcelona, 1947.

Torres Balbás, Leopoldo. *Arquitectura gótica, Ars Hispaniae,* Vol. VII. Madrid, 1952.

Varela Jácome, Benito. *Historia de la literatura gallega.* Santiago de Compostela, 1951.

Vázquez de Parga, Luis, José María Lacarra, and Juan Uría Rúi. *Las Peregrinaciones a Santiago de Compostela.* 3 Vols. Madrid, 1948–49.

Villaamil y Castro, José. *La catedral de Santiago, breve descripción histórica.* Madrid, 1909.

———. *Descripción histórico-artístico-arqueológica de la catedral de Santiago.* Lugo, 1866.

Whitehill, Walter Muir. *Spanish Romanesque Architecture of the Eleventh Century.* London, 1941.

Zepedano y Carnero, José María. *Historia y descripción arqueológica de la basílica compostelana.* Lugo, 1870.

Journals

These journals contain many useful and important studies

(see especially studies by Manuel Chamoso Lamas and José Manuel Pita Andrade).

Archivo español de arte, Instituto Diego Velázquez, Consejo Superior de Investigaciones Científicas, Madrid.

Boletín, Sociedad español de excursiones, Madrid.

Compostellanum, Revista trimestral de la Archidiocesis de Santiago de Compostela, Sección de Estudios Jacobeos. Santiago de Compostela.

Cuadernos de Estudios Gallegos, Instituto Padre Sarmiento de Estudios Gallegos, Consejo Superior de Investigaciones Científicas, Santiago de Compostela.

Index

Alcantara, Order of: 28
Alfonso II (the Chaste): 7, 15, 132; first pilgrim to Santiago, 8
Alfonso III: 8, 11, 12, 47
Alfonso VI: 17, 53, 64–67, 81, 91, 92, 107, 128–30
Alfonso (Raimundez) VII: 24, 66, 81, 86, 111
Alfonso VIII: 87
Alfonso IX: 28, 87, 88, 151
Alfonso XI: 157
Alfonso of Aragón: 24, 66, 81, 91
Almanzor: 8. 9, 12, 155
Almohades: 87, 88, 137, 139
Almoravides: 64, 86
Anastasius (disciple of St. James): 7, 8
Aragón, Spain: 23, 52, 66, 81, 84, 87, 90, 156
Architecture: 45–49, 51–52, 131–33; Paraiso, 23, 38, 43; fortifications, 35–37; streets, 35, 38; gates, 36–38; parish churches, 38, 45; aqueduct, 38–39, 123, 132; in Santiago de Compostela, 40–63; houses, 40–41, 122; palace of Gelmírez, 43–44, 70; *see also* Cathedral of Santiago de Compostela
Arias, Juan (archbishop): 156

Asturias, Spain: 19; architecture, 9, 12, 13, 46, 47, 51, 82, 131, 132
Augustinians: 17
Avila, Juan de: 160
Avila, Spain: 37

Banquets: 44, 127–28
Basques: 31–33
Benedictines: 17
Bernardo (treasurer): 39, 53, 82, 108–10, 132
Bordelais, France: 30
Bridge building: 25
Brugos, Spain: 21, 33
Burgundy, France: 7
Byzantium: 18, 46, 163

Calatrava, Order of: 28
Calixtus II (Pope): 19, 24, 66, 80; sermons, 50–51; call to crusade, 84–86
Cántigas (Hymns to the Virgin Mary): 151
Casas y Novoa, Fernando (architect): 161
Castile, Spain: 16, 65, 79, 83, 86, 90, 102, 149, 156–59
Catalonia, Spain: 19, 51, 64, 87, 91
Cathedral of Santiago de Compostela: 48–63, 69, 82, 132–40; ear-

lier buildings on site, 9–13, 36; fortified, 35; altars, 48, 59–62; additions, 53, 138; lamps, 62; burned in 1117, 69–70; administration, 99–101; archives, 103–104, 132, 144; *catedral vieja,* 137

Chamoso Lamas, Manuel: 9, 10

Charlemagne: 32

Chartres, France, cathedral school: 142

Chaucer: 29

Church furniture: 47

Cid, el (Rodrigo Díaz de Vilar): 64, 92

Cistercians: 46, 139

Civil disorders: 37, 41, 44, 67, 69–78, 94

Clavejo, Battle of: 8, 88

Clement VII (Pope): 156

Clothing: 126–27, 129–30

Cluny, France, and Cluniacs: 17, 65, 133, 144

Codax, Martin (troubadour): 152

Codex Calixtinus: 6, 19, 24, 40, 51, 151; quotations, 27, 50, 84–86, 104–105, 115–21, 124–25, 128–30

Codex Calixtinus, Book V *(Pilgrims' Guide):* 19–20, 44, 53, 133, 135–36; quotations, 20–34, 36–37, 39–40, 48, 50–51, 53–63, 100–101

Colonia, Juan de (architect): 159

Conant, Kenneth John: 53

Conques, France: 133

Constantine: 16, 46

Crusade: 83–87, 147

Diocletian: 7

Drake, Sir Francis: 9, 160

Drama: 148

Ebro River, Spain: 23

Economy: 89, 97–98, 101–22; trade, 40; mint, 83, 107; guilds, 105; fairs, 110–11; prices in 1133, 111–14

Education: 44, 99, 142–47

Estella, Spain: 21

Enrique de Trastámara: 157

Ferdinand II: 28, 58, 87, 88, 136, 139

Ferdinand III: 84, 87, 155, 157

Fonseca, Alonso de (I, II, and III, archbishops): 38, 158–59

García de Santa María, Alonso (bishop of Burgos): 159

Gascony, France: 31

Gelmírez, Diego: 9, 17, 24, 35, 41, 44, 64–83, 107–111, 126, 127, 131–33, 136, 141–44, 147–48, 152, 154, 157; civil wars, 69–78, 94; reforms, 78–79, 98–101; navy, 82–83; trade, 82–83; government, 98–101; mint, 107; donations to cathedral, 126, 141–42

Giraldo (Gerardo): 143, 148

Gómez, Suero (archbishop): 157

Gudesteiz, Pedro (archbishop): 87, 136

Guilds: 102–106

Henry of Lorraine, King of Portugal: 65

Historia Compostelana: 19, 44, 66, 68, 69, 78, 79, 81, 105, 111, 125, 126, 140, 143, 147, 148; quotations, 69–78, 95–98, 108–10, 111–14, 141–42

Holy Land, pilgrims to: 14

Holy Sepulchre: 16

Hospices and hospitals: 17, 42–43; Paris, 158

INDEX

Innkeepers: 29, 40, 114–18, 121
Innocent II: 80
Iria, Spain: 8, 77
Isabel of Castile: 158, 159

Jaca, Spain: 21, 133, 134
Jet: 105–106
Jubilee: 88

Knights: 27; Santiago, 28, 83; Cáceres, 28; Alcantara, 28; Calatrava, 28

Lancaster, Duke of: 157
Landes, France: 30
Legends: 5–7, 14, 22
León, San Isidoro, Pantheon of the Kings: 140
León, Spain: 19, 22, 28, 33, 52, 90, 133, 134
Liber Sancti Jacobi: see Codex Calixtinus, Pilgrims' Guide
Lily: 124–25
Lombardy, Italy: 46, 51
López Ferreiro, Antonio: 10, 44
Louis VI of France: 24
Lupa: 6

Magic: 140
Masonry: 22, 25, 45–46
Master Matthew: 58, 103–104, 136–40, 153
Maximilian of Austria (archbishop): 160
Medical practice: 42–43, 123
Merchants: *see* economy; attacks on, 92; fraudulent practices, 114–21
Mezonzo, Pedro (bishop): 150
Military orders: 28, 83, 126
Mint: 83, 107
Miracles: 5–9, 26–27, 29
Monte del Gozo, Spain: 35, 36
Montserrat, Spain: 19

Moors: 7, 17, 18, 35, 46, 51, 64, 86–87, 127, 131, 134, 137, 163; music, 152–53
Moscoso, Rodrigo de (archbishop): 157
Mozarabs: 46; architecture, 82; music, 152
Muñiz, Pedro (archbishop): 88, 155
Music: 51, 150–53; instruments, 152–53

Napoleonic Wars: 162
Navarre, Spain: 52, 84, 90
Navarrese: 23, 32, 33
Norway: 18
Núñez, Aryas (poet): 150

Ordoñiz II: 67
Oviedo, Spain: San Julian de los Prados, 12; cathedral, 19

Padrón, Spain: 6, 18, 37, 92
Palencia, decrees of council of 1129: 78–79
Pamplona, Spain: 21
Paris, France: 144, 158
Pedro, the Cruel: 157
Peláez, Diego (bishop): 80
Petrus (bridge builder): 25
Picaud, Aymery: 17, 19
Pilgrimage: 14–16; early routes, 17; sea routes, 18; detours to other shrines, 19; public safety, 26; prohibited in seventeenth century, 161
Pilgrimage church: 45–52
Pilgrimage road: 17–24, 30–34
Pilgrimage style: 15
Pilgrims: 14, 26, 155–59; dangers, 23–24, 27, 29, 31–33; protection, 26, 79, 97; fraud, 114–21
Pilgrims' Guide: see Codex Calixtinus
Pillar (Zaragoza): 19

175

Pirates: 18, 35, 83
Pistoia, Italy: 9, 143
Poetry: 148–51
Poitiers, France: 26, 27, 30
Poitou, France: 17, 30
Porter, Arthur Kingsley: 15, 133
Pórtico de la Gloria: 53, 58,
   136–40, 148, 152, 153, 159;
   inscription, 138
Portugal: 10, 12, 33, 65, 86, 156,
   158; poetry, 149
Processions: 128–30
Puente la Reina, Spain: 21

Rainero of Pistoia (scholar): 143
Raymond Berenquer IV: 64, 86
Raymond of Burgundy: 65, 80, 91
Recreation: 127–28
Relics: 8, 9, 10, 47, 160, 162–63
Road building: 14, 24–25
Robert of Salerno (scholar): 143
Roger of Sicily: 18
Rome, Italy, and Romans in Spain:
   10–11, 80, 133, 134; tomb, 12;
   pilgrims to, 14; roads, 24; build-
   ing, 46, 51
Roncesvalles, Spain: 18, 21, 32

Saint Denis, France, abbey of: 46
Saint Dominic: 155
Saint Ferdinand: *see* Ferdinand III
Saint Francis of Assisi: 155
Saint Gilles, France: 30
Saint James (Apostle): 5–6, 15;
   miracles, 5–9, 59, 143; tomb, 6,
   7, 10, 11; patron of all Spain, 76
Saint Lazarus (hospital): 43
Saint Louis of France: 155
Saint Mary: 29, 46
Saintonge, France: 17, 30
Saint Peter, tomb in Rome: 16
Salve Regina (hymn): 150
Sancho, Prince (son of Alfonso VI):
   66

San Clemente, Juan de (archbishop):
   160
Santiago de Compostela: 35ff.;
   Roman site, 10–11, 36; education, 44, 99, 142–47; music, 51,
   151–53; civic government, 68,
   94–98, 102; justice, 92–96; notaries, 96, 107–108; medicine,
   123–25; public welfare, 125–26;
   the Christian Mecca, 131; sixteenth-century building, 161–62
Santiago matamoros: 8
Santo Domingo de la Calzada: 14,
   25
Santo Domingo de Silos, monastery:
   19, 140
Sarela River, Spain: 35, 36
Sar River, Spain: 35, 36
Scallop shell: 6, 15, 89; vendors,
   104–106
Sculpture: 133–40; "Pilgrimage
   style," 133–36; Master Matthew,
   136–40
Sigurd, King of the Isles and of Norway: 18
Social classes: 91–95; serfs freed in
   city, 67
Stuart, James, of England: 162
Suárez, Pedro (archbishop): 79, 83,
   88, 89, 131, 139, 150, 155
Suevi: 7, 11
Suger, Abbot: 46, 82, 138, 139
Sumptuary arts: 59–62, 105–106,
   109–10, 129–30, 140–42

Taifas: 86
Tarragona, Spain: 11
Teodomiro (bishop): 8, 15, 59
Teresa of Portugal (daughter of
   Alfonso VI): 65
Textiles: 128–30, 140–41
Theodosius (disciple of St. James):
   7, 8

INDEX

Tierra de Santiago: 98, 131

Toledo, Spain: 64, 65, 83; archbishop, 65, 80, 81, 83, 109

Toulouse, France: 9, 20, 30, 133, 135; church of St. Sernin, 52

Traba, Count of: 18, 66, 92

Tumbo A: 103–104, 132

Tumbo B: 144

Uclés, Battle of: 66

Urban II (Pope): 13

Urban VI (Pope): 156

Urraca, Queen (daughter of Alfonso VI): 25, 65–66, 69–74, 77, 141

Vatican Cancionero: 150

Vega y Verdugo, José de (architect): 161

Vézelay, France: 20, 30

Vikings: 7, 8, 17

Visigoths: 46, 51

Votos de Santiago: 88, 97, 160, 162

William of Aquitaine: 150

Zaragoza, Spain: 83